IN WAR'S SHADOW

At the Edge of the Cold War: America's Last Stand

Rick Waddell

Jacksonville, Florida ♦ Herndon, Virginia
www.Fortis-Publishing.com

IN WARS SHADOW

At the Edge of the Cold War: America's Last Stand

By Rick Waddell

ISBN 978-0-9846371-2-6 (trade paperback version)

Published by Fortis Publishing
Jacksonville, Florida—Herndon, Virginia
www.Fortis-Publishing.com

Manufactured in the United States of America

Previously published January 1993 by Ivy Books/Ballantine Books. This Fortis edition includes updated and new material.

Cover photo credit: Aerial view of Palmerola – source Wikipedia.
All other photos, courtesy the author.

DEDICATION

I dedicate this book to three men who taught me so much about leadership, soldiering, service, and humanity:

Command Sergeant Major Otto V. Moore
Sergeant Major James L. Wise
First Sergeant James W. Taylor

Whatever I might do in the Army, I will owe in large measure to these men.

Acknowledgments

There are several people to whom I owe debts of gratitude for making this publication possible.

First and most important are my wife and children, who had to endure my writing struggles.

Next is Andrew Barros, a true intellect who is also very much a man firmly planted in the practical world. He prodded me to take my diary to a publisher back in 1989.

Finally, I have to mention all of the soldiers with whom I have been privileged to serve. Their quiet struggles, constant dedication, and occasional human failures prompted me to start a diary to record at least a part of their history.

To these go only the credits and none of the inevitable errors.

Table of Contents

i – Prologue 2011

v – Prelude

1 – Chapter 1 Preparation

9 – Chapter 2 Assignment to Honduras

15 – Chapter 3 The Country

26 – Chapter 4 Palmerola Air Base

42 – Chapter 5 Settling In

64 – Chapter 6 Deployments and Exercises

99 – Chapter 7 Ahuas Tara '86

135 – Chapter 8 Morale, Welfare, and Recreation

147 – Chapter 9 The Adversarial Relationship

160 – Chapter 10 Going Home

165 – Epilogue

176 – Postscript 2011

181 – Appendix A: Terrorist Attacks on U.S. Troops in Honduras, 1986-1990

183 – Appendix B: Balance of Power in Central America, 1986

185 – Appendix C: Major U.S. Exercise and Deployments TO Honduras, 1983-1986

189 – About the Author

189 – Notes

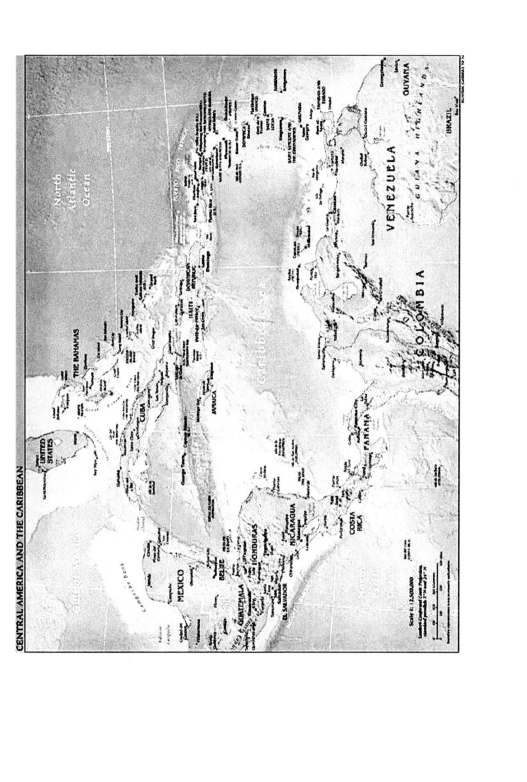
CENTRAL AMERICA AND THE CARIBBEAN

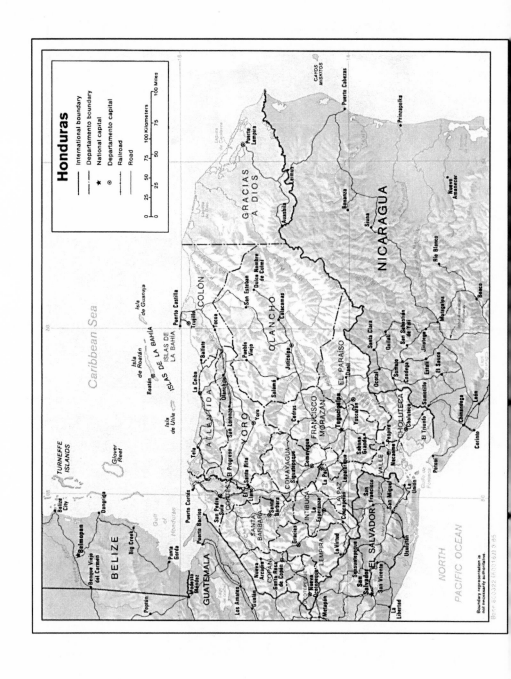

Honduras

- International boundary
- - - Departamento boundary
★ National capital
⊛ Departamento capital
+-+-+ Railroad
——— Road

0 25 50 75 100 Kilometers
0 25 50 75 100 Miles

Caribbean Sea

BELIZE

Belize City
Dangriga
Big Creek
Belmopan
Punta Gorda
Belize Viejo del Carmen
Melchor de Mencos
TURNEFFE ISLANDS
Glover Reef
Peptun

GUATEMALA

Los Amates
Puerto Barrios

Gulf of Honduras

Isla de Utila
Isla de Roatán
Isla de Guanaja
ISLAS DE LA BAHIA
ISLAS DE LA BAHIA

Puerto Cortés
San Pedro Sula
El Limón
Tela
La Ceiba
Olanchito
Trujillo
Puerto Castilla
Balfate

COLON

Laguna de Caratasca
Puerto Lempira
CAYOS MISKITOS
Puerto Lempira

GRACIAS A DIOS

Auasbila
Leimus

San Esteban
Dulce Nombre de Culmí
Catacamas
Bonanza
Siuna
Río Blanco

NICARAGUA

Prinzapolka
Puerto Cabezas
Nuevo Amanecer

ATLANTIDA
YORO
El Progreso
Santa Rita
Yoro
Salamá
Pueblo Viejo
Juticalpa
OLANCHO

SANTA BARBARA
Santa Bárbara
San Lorenzo
Morazán
Cedros
Comayagua
Siguatepeque
COMAYAGUA

Nueva Arcapán
Santa Rosa de Copán
COPAN
Gracias
La Esperanza
INTIBUCA
LEMPIRA
La Virtud
Metapán

EL SALVADOR
San Salvador
San Vicente
La Libertad
Usulután
San Miguel
San Francisco
La Paz
LA PAZ
Marcala
Concepción
Sabanagrande
Pespire
Nacaome
VALLE
Langue
La Unión
Gulf of Fonseca
Potosí
Choluteca
CHOLUTECA
El Triunfo
San Marcos de Colón
Corinto
Chinandega
León

FRANCISCO MORAZAN
Tegucigalpa
Yuscarán
EL PARAISO
Danlí
Yuscarán
Ocotal
Somoto
Condega
Quilalí
Jalapa
San Sebastián de Yalí
Santa Clara
Estelí
El Sauce
Matagalpa

NORTH
PACIFIC OCEAN

Boundary representation is not necessarily authoritative.

Base 803322 (A00156) 8-95

PROLOGUE 2011

Why revise and re-issue a book so long after the events?

We are now two decades removed from the U.S. and allied victory in the Cold War, caused by the collapse of the Berlin Wall and the Iron Curtain. In Korea, Vietnam, and Afghanistan (for the Soviets) the Cold War became hot and bloody, rising to mid-intensity levels. For the most part, the Cold War was waged via standing forces conducting periodic exercises to demonstrate political will and military capacity, and through the readiness of air defense and nuclear missile systems to defend or retaliate against any sudden attack. We tend to forget, though, that in the more than four decades of that conflict, the actions generally happened on the periphery away from the main front along the "inter-German border" in Europe, or the secondary front along the Demilitarized Zone in Korea. These actions often happened "in the shadows" along this periphery through intelligence and counterintelligence operations, and through U.S. and Soviet support for proxies in conflicts that might have begun over local or internal disputes. This support from both sides was generally both economic and military. The locations were in those areas of the world described variously as the Third World, the Lesser Developed Countries, or Developing Countries in Latin America, Africa, and Asia.

Why does it matter? By the 1980s, a school of thought had arisen that essentially treated the U.S. and the Soviets as morally equivalent and equally responsible for the Cold War. The broad lines of such thinking might accept that the Soviet Union was heavy-handed in Eastern Europe, but this was understandable given the historic invasion routes that passed through the region and the recent staggering Soviet losses in World War II. Outside of Europe, in this line of thinking, when the Soviets lent support to communist revolutionary movements in Asia, Africa or Latin America, such support was not determinative of the success of these movements which were seen as natural manifestations of nationalist or anti-colonial sentiments; moreover, the Soviets were often just responding to prior U.S. meddling. Besides, the U.S. could not be seen as morally superior in any way, since it had problems with civil rights, unemployment, the lack of free healthcare, rampant materialistic consumerism, and had historically supported tyrants, especially in Latin America. Since the Americans were no better than the Soviets (and maybe even worse to some critics), the best possible U.S. foreign policy would be one of mutual recognition and accommodation with the Soviets and other communist states. Part of this desired policy shift would be an acceptance by the U.S. of the basic legitimacy of the communist states as valid expressions of their peoples' collective desires. As such, since these states were delivering basic economic goods in a just manner, even if at the expense of some of the political freedoms that the U.S. might find more desirable, they would endure. Any acceptance of the basic legitimacy of communist states would, of course, call into question the basic U.S. policy of containment upon which much of the defense establishment was built, and would completely undermine as futile any notion of "roll back" or "victory." Thus, the U.S. need not get involved combating communist insurgencies, even if the insurgencies were supported actively or indirectly by communist countries. The U.S. might even go so far as to recognize that it had been on the "wrong side of history" in many of these conflicts.

Sadly, for this school of thought, the Cold War did end, and suddenly, when the supposedly contented peoples of the Soviet Bloc of Eastern Europe tore down the Iron Curtain and the economically moribund Soviet Union chose not to respond violently. Worse, the newly liberated nations wanted into the Western economic, political, and defense structures that were supposedly no better than – and perhaps even more unjust economically – than the Soviet Bloc. Worse still, many of the other nations that had lived under Soviet enlightenment for more than 70 years also rose up and seceded from the Soviet Union. With the economic and then political collapse of the Soviets, Castro's Cuba could no longer afford to maintain its large troop formations in Africa, or to maintain its sponsorship of revolutionary movements in the Americas. Given the chance to vote in free and fair elections, the Chileans emerged from the right-wing dictatorship of Pinochet to choose a moderate government, and the Nicaraguans rejected the Soviet and Cuban-backed Sandinistas.

The Marxist FMLN in El Salvador shortly thereafter sought peace. Even in China, after the violent repression at Tiananmen Square in 1989, the Communist Party began to allow astounding market reforms in the economy, even though retaining a monopoly on authoritarian political control in the hands of the Party. In a time span of months, given the barest of chances to choose, many tens of millions rejected the very systems that so many Western intellectuals and politicians had come to accept as inevitable and enduring. The reversal was stunning.

We are now engaged in a new ideological struggle with the multi-ethnic adherents of a fanatical strain of Islam – a new "long war" as some call it. These fanatics use the tools of terrorism and insurgency to advance their agenda. And, we are beginning to hear some of the same arguments today that were heard in the 1980s: the U.S. must accept and accommodate…Maybe the situations is really our own fault…Maybe the U.S. and its foreign policies or its domestic life-style were at least an accessory to the 9-11 attacks….The U.S. cannot win and cannot hope to impose liberal democratic values…or we hear that "those people just aren't ready for democracy…."

That is why I think re-issuing this book is important. This account of six months of actions of a small ad hoc force on the periphery of the Cold War is merely a representation of the larger context of the time, when acidic domestic political controversy swirled around these U.S. actions, when U.S. resolve and its armed forces were still in question after the self-imposed defeats in Indochina the decade before. In the glaring clarity of hindsight, perhaps it was the U.S. political perseverance and the re-building of the American military in the 1980s - which ran contrary to the intellectual currents of the period - that provided the basis for the victory of the Western democracies in the Cold War. Reading this account now might offer some lessons from the past, and hope for the future.

Some cautions. I wrote this book based on a diary I kept as a young officer. Twenty-five years later, much of what I wrote then strikes me as brash and hard since I now empathize more with the older characters. Nonetheless, I will leave my younger self to tell the story he recorded at the time (although I will no doubt cringe at certain points), changing mainly the verb tenses and adding some tidbits to the historical context. However, in this revised version I have removed most of the names that I included in the original, an indication of the softness, or the empathy, that being older brings. One learns a great deal of humility with increased age, and whatever shortcomings we had as individuals or soldiers in the mid-1980s in Honduras need not plague us now so long afterwards.

PRELUDE

The old colonel, a veteran of World War II and whose grandfather had fought with the Union Army, descended the ramp of the C-141 Starlifter. A young captain walked hurriedly up to meet him but stopped short at catching the old man's pinched eyebrows, his distant, slowly turning gaze.

"Oh my God," the colonel muttered.

"What's wrong, sir? Are you all right?" the captain asked, not really knowing what to do.

"The damn plane made a wrong turn, Captain, a wrong turn in time. I'm back twenty years. I've been here before. This—" He made a sweeping gesture with his arm towards the base camp, "—is Da Nang ..."

Such was the power that Palmerola Air Base (PAB) often had on Vietnam veterans. Vietnam – the collective fear of the memory – was constantly referenced by those serving at Palmerola, those visiting, and those writing and reporting on Central American events.

On any given day in the 1980s, over two million men and women quietly served their country in the uniformed military services. As general peace reigned in the world, it was easy to forget that war raged almost continuously on what might be called the periphery of the two blocs headed by our own country and the Soviet Union. Occasionally the U.S. armed services were called into action.

In Central America where the threat was closest to our own borders, we engaged in a political-military dance of the strangest and increasingly familiar sort—a low-intensity conflict. The threat from an expanding body of ideas—an ideology—was vague; the threat from the military power accompanying the ideas was easier to measure but did not seem sufficient to many to warrant the American response. That very response seemed a half-hearted affair. It was on-again, off-again. Small exercises were held, then big ones, then small ones. Aid was voted, then cut, then voted again. Clandestine operations were only part of the process, but their presence convinced too many that "covert ops" were the main part. All of this is fitting for a style of conflict that has been called a "war in the shadows."

Into all of this went a mere fraction of a fraction of America's military might. Yet over the course of the '80s, close to one hundred thousand soldiers served in Central America, a dribble at a time. More than twenty-seven thousand of those came from the Reserve and National Guard forces. Many, if not most, of those forces came from the combat support and the combat service support branches—in other words, these were not the teeth, but the tail of the armed services. All of these people were also volunteers.

Because we had been at general peace for so long and because we had to attract volunteers in very large numbers, the service life became more humane and endurable than it had ever been. Some would maintain that it became too easy; that we pampered the troops too much in order to attract new volunteers and to keep reenlistment rates high; that this treatment could make our forces too soft to engage in the horrors of war, especially if we had to fight at the spur of the moment without a train-up period. Such thinking became quite prevalent in the 1980s, and as a young officer, I tended to agree with this assessment; however, those of us who perceived softness should have heeded the warning of Martin Van Creveld:

> Looking back, one suspects that the view that "modern youth" is soft has its origins in the last tree-man's forlornly decrying his son's unfortunate move into the comparative luxury of caves. It has not prevented any number of wars' taking place since, and it surely will not prevent many more from taking place in the future. . . . When everything is said and done, nothing that has happened in recent years gives the slightest indication that modern man's attitude to and suitability for warfare differs appreciably from that of previous generations.[1]

The only reason for writing this book is to provide an account of some of the activities of the United States armed services in Central America in the mid-1980s. It was a story not often seen in the headlines, and when it was, generally the reporting was of low quality. One day the full story will be written by someone far more qualified as a scholar than I am. Perhaps by recording my observations and experiences, that job will be made easier.

I have tried to be as faithful to the facts as my memory allows, and I did keep a diary. In this revised edition, most names have been changed. Naturally, the conversations are not in any way to be taken as word-for-word but are my attempts at reconstruction. I have also added at the beginning and the end a certain amount of context, so that the reader will understand the background, the governing doctrine, and the aftermath of the main part of the story. As well, throughout the account, brief descriptions of events occurring in the "outside" world provide another essential element of context.

There are two ways of looking at a military operation. The first is akin to a backwoods farmer flying for the first time over a major city. The rural observer marvels at how orderly life appears, with all the buildings lined up in neat rectangular rows and ships docking and traffic flowing, all in regular patterns. The thought of what it must take to light, heat, feed, and water the multitudes below would certainly astound the farmer. The second method requires spending some time on the ground in the city itself. Then, all the street garbage, chaos, crime, soot, and occasional inhumanity of the place would be readily apparent.

If one reads about the capture of the Ludendorff Bridge at Remagen in 1945, the story is likely to be written from the first vantage point—amazement at the luck of the American forces and their subsequent efforts to drive floating bridges across the Rhine under heavy German artillery fire in order to deliver the final blow to Nazi Germany. Yet, in one popular movie account of the same action, the scene is far less uplifting because it employs the second lens. The American soldiers appear far more hard-bitten and ill disciplined than they do heroic. The pivotal company grade officer is shiftless, leaving his troops to be led by an insubordinate corporal. The corporal later punches the major who orders the unit onto the bridge.

The story I'm about to tell will use both lenses as the occasion demands.

The story is not always uplifting. In fact, some of the vignettes ought to cause the average taxpayer some concern. One important point to keep in mind, though, is that we were not at war. In military parlance, the events described were "operations short of war" in a "low-intensity conflict." Hence, the all-volunteer, peacetime military was the star of the show, the show being the longest and largest use of American might outside of Europe or Korea since the Paris Peace Accords of 1973 and before the Gulf War. The stage was provided primarily by the Honduran Republic.

In the 1980s and early 1990s, the American military was a paradox in many ways. Our people saw the military when it jumped into a short operation like Grenada or Panama, or they watched as the troops captured the screen for a few days as they did in DESERT SHIELD and DESERT STORM. The public heard far more about the latest procurement scandal in the Pentagon or the latest spy ring, but the fact that more than two million service members were on duty at any given time generally escaped view. We had a better understanding of what it was like to have been in the Army of the frontier days, World War II, or Vietnam than we did of the life in the armed forces of the 1980s. Much of that life, when in garrison, was sedentary and safe, little removed from civilian occupations. On the other hand, when deployed, the days were long, arduous, and dangerous, although much more so for soldiers and Marines in the combat arms – the "teeth" – than those in the supporting arms – the "tail."

It would be easy to say that the Army in the 1980s was mostly a garrison force, a nine-to-five occupation, or a giant social-welfare program as some of its critics of the time described it. Undoubtedly, it exhibited many of these characteristics. Yet perhaps the human failings exceeded those of the institution. The Army in a pluralistic, democratic society will reflect that society, for good or evil.

The hodgepodge force of individual augmentees that I served with in Honduras was representative of the best and the worst of the Army and the Air Force of that period, the way we organized for war, and of how we waged peace. Too few of the Navy were present to tell. There were many caring, dedicated professionals at all ranks and not a little deadwood. Counterpoised to the caring and dedication were attitudes that smacked more of TV than reality, tunnel vision rather than perception, civilian bureaucracy rather than things military, self-centeredness rather than the long-suffering self-sacrifice that America has often demanded from its military professionals in peacetime.

However, whatever the faults, what the American forces accomplished in Honduras or in much of Central America since 1983 cannot be dismissed as poorly done or unimportant. Many critics of our Low Intensity Conflict doctrine, past and present, claimed that the American military never got it quite right.[2] Part of the reason for this book is to show that we may have had it more right than is commonly thought, if we catch a conflict early enough. Perhaps that is the key variable, taking preventive measures rather than having to wage a counterinsurgency operation after the fact.

Who can evaluate the actual effects that shows of force and civic assistance programs had on the minds of the El Salvadoran FMLN or the Nicaraguan FSLN and their main supporters in the Soviet Bloc? Yet, the roads, bridges, schools, and airstrips built, the wells drilled, and the medical services dispensed had an enduring effect serving as a foundation for continued U.S. support for democracy, security, and development in the region. In the mid-1980s, we may not have done our duty as efficiently, or in as disciplined a manner as we should have, but we did well enough, and did it for good ends. Here is at least part of the story, a small chapter in the continuing history of American arms and American involvement in Central America.

1
PREPARATION

The end for which a soldier is recruited, clothed, armed, and trained, the whole object of his sleeping, eating, drinking, and marching is simply that he should fight at the right place and the right time.

—Clausewitz, *On War*

Just about every other book in the Thomas Jefferson Elementary library in tiny Bentonville, Arkansas, seemed to treat a topic of military history. All the heroes were there—Washington, Lee, Grant, Sherman, Pershing, MacArthur, Patton, and Eisenhower. So many of them had gone to a magnificent, grueling place called West Point. This was just before Vietnam seemed to kill heroes, military or otherwise.

The schoolrooms in Thomas Jefferson often had historical panoramas posted above the blackboards. One had summaries of the lives of each American president. Another had a time line depicting the pivotal points in American history. The lofty thoughts and ideals of Washington, Lincoln, Roosevelt, and Kennedy looked down on our labors. Short descriptions of Valley Forge, Yorktown, Gettysburg, Saint-Mihiel, Normandy, and Inchon were handy to fill wandering eyes. This was just before the education establishment stopped teaching so much U.S. history.

On the playgrounds, at recess, groups of young boys chose sides. They argued over who was going to be the Germans—the losers. Then, the wars began. The great leaders led their troops into mock battles, employing tactics of surprise, diversion, envelopment, but most often, the preferred method was the frontal assault. And the dead never stayed dead for long. Occasionally, someone would ask,

"Hey, who's America fightin' now, anyway?"

Another would reply, "Dummy, don't you watch the news? We're fighting the *Vi-et-nuh-meese!*"

"Who're they?"

"Shoot, I don't know . . . just a different kind of German, I guess."

Then came the hippies, the protests, drugs on the playground, the generation gap, and fashionable anti-Americanism—all of this on top of the normal pains of adolescence—sports, girls, and being "cool." This time also brought scenes of disaster—fleeing multitudes, the embassy roof in Saigon, helicopters being pushed extravagantly over the sides of aircraft carriers, Mayagüez. The old verities found in the books at Thomas Jefferson seemed far away.

* * *

As I walked into the Bentonville high school gym on a cold December day in 1976 the coach came over and said, "How would you like to play football for the Military Academy at West Point? I got a call from them today, and they're interested in you."

"Sure, Coach. That would be great . . . ," was what I managed to stammer out as memories flooded my mind, memories from the books I had read as a child. West Point—the words had a magic ring to them, even in the cynical seventies. To walk, or rather march, where so many great Americans had marched; to play football on the same fields where Ike had played were the library dreams of the kid who read too much. I had almost forgotten those dreams.

Eighteen months later on the Plain at the United States Military Academy (USMA), I participated in my first parade. It occurred at the end of our first day of cadet basic training. The class of 1982 stood row upon row, 1,397 strong, clad in the white shirts and gray trousers we had only just learned to put on a few hours before. We wore no hats.

Like the farmer in the airplane flying over the huge city, the casual observer would have marveled at the order of it all as we went through *Forward march, Mark time, Present arms, Column right,* and *Column left*—commands we had been drilling on for several hours. The astute observer, one with military experience, might have remarked, "Well, not bad, I guess, for the first day." I, for one, almost cried at the thought of dreams coming true.

Two other memories loom in importance from plebe year, one

specific, the other collective. West Point has incredible beauty. In basic training, we reported to our physical training formations just after dawn. As we assembled on the concrete apron that skirted the parade field, fog often still covered the Plain. As plebes were forbidden to talk, the formations were quiet and eerie. Looking out into the beautiful fog that covered what I considered hallowed ground, it was quite easy to imagine hearing the mutterings of bygone years, the voices of the historical giants as well as those who had surrounded them in their youth. Perhaps it was just the Academy lore we were forced to learn, or maybe even the illicit whispers of my classmates, but the feeling was there. Had those young Americans been cynical, brash, carefree, too? Or were they possessed of a surety and drive that escaped my generation? Could they reasonably foresee the years of war, turmoil, and bloodshed that awaited them? Given the pattern of their lives, what might lie ahead for us?

The collective memory from plebe year is one of discipline—the discipline that West Point was justifiably famous for. The words that come to mind are "harsh," "dry," "bone-crushing," and "repetitive." And "fear"—the fear of failure and the inevitable disgrace that it would bring. Fears held in check most of our natural adolescent tendencies to rebel or to act stupid in the ways of most freshmen elsewhere. West Point held us to the standards and the beliefs we professed to want to uphold.

The rest of the years at West Point were less distinctive. We had internalized the values, learned the discipline. The time passed in a blur of classes, summer military training, physical-training tests, football games, and the occasional humorous event.

One such event occurred during my junior year ("cow year" in cadet slang). It was indicative of the climate of the times. West Point, it seems, had been accused of turning out social misfits—officers who did not know how to interact with their civilian peers. This was seen to be a direct result of the cloistered nature of the Academy. The Academy environment must have irritated those who felt that true adults were produced only when a post-adolescent is given enough rope to hang himself. Hence, beginning my plebe year, cadets could buy alcohol and experience drunkenness. Then came the cry to allow cadets more free time on the weekends to unwind. Finally, there was the desire to get away from the staid military atmosphere of the place by allowing cadets to dress in civilian clothes—I guess the Military Academy was just too military for some tastes. It was this last innovation that produced the humor.

The Academy employed a trio of ladies as hostesses. One of their jobs was to teach cadets the fine arts of etiquette, or "cadetiquette" as it was called. They even published a pamphlet covering all the important points. Unfortunately, what the pamphlet described as appropriate civilian attire included a sketch of a fellow who looked like a gangster character out of a Bogart movie, complete with fedora. Such fashions were hopelessly out of style. Yet, the Academy had to have a policy covering civilian attire. Eventually it filtered down to the cadets. Informal attire consisted of coat and tie. Casual attire consisted of slacks and a shirt with a collar. A sweater and tie were also suggested. Blue jeans were absolutely not allowed.

The blue-jean policy caused the first problem. This was the era of designer jeans—simple jeans with high- powered trade names like Gitano or Calvin Klein. Some went for as high as fifty dollars a pair, an enormous price in those days. Once a cadet was permitted to wear civvies, why not let him or her wear the latest fashion? Sure enough, a modification to the policy came down—we could wear designer jeans, or jeans that were actually blue and not faded, as long as they had an ironed crease in the leg—the perfect marriage of the modern military and designer clothes.

The next inevitable modification soon followed. Different regions of the country define "formal" differently. Those from the Southwest liked to wear cowboy boots with their coats and ties. Initially, the keepers of decorum declared this to be in bad taste. Then, some cadet exercised his constitutional right to complain to Congress, in this case Sen. John Tower of Texas, the ranking Republican on the Senate Armed Services Committee. One day a Xeroxed copy of a letter appeared on my company bulletin board. Senator Tower had sent it to our commandant, stating in simple terms that cowboy boots were considered quite fashionable by several million of his constituents. The policy rapidly changed—the boots were now acceptable, provided they were in good repair, etc.

The civvies farce is illustrative of what can happen when a military organization seeks to modernize a little too rapidly or seeks to conform to the principles of a well-managed business, or seeks to follow the latest fad. The old touchstones are gone. Confusion reigns, and people, especially in America, start to think of the Army only as a good place to get a little education or maybe some vocational training. These forces of change were particularly strong after the Vietnam War ended and the volunteer Army was created.

My first real experience with that Army came during the summer between my sophomore and junior years at West Point, in June and July 1980. I was sent to Fort Campbell, Kentucky, to serve as a platoon leader in an Air Defense Artillery (ADA) battery belonging to the fabled 101st Division. The Army had recently designated the division part of the Rapid Deployment Force. Supposedly, the unit had to have troops ready to fight within a few hours of notice.

What I found was disheartening. My battery was short one officer and several NCOs, so the unit was glad to see me. My platoon sergeant was a staff sergeant (E6) with eighteen years in service. The platoon was understrength by 25 percent, so we could not man all of our Vulcan ADA guns—one constantly went unattended. My best gun section leader was a well-known pothead who had recently been busted two grades from staff sergeant to specialist fourth class (E4). He also had a permanent physical "profile," an exemption from any physical training or heavy duty. It was also well known that he had finagled the profile and was, in fact, in perfect health. Another section leader was a French Canadian who had trouble with the English language. Several of my men belonged to a clique of Hispanic soldiers that operated as a sort of barracks mafia, dealing in drugs. These soldiers, the farthest thing from what I expected, were the inheritors of those who had fought at Yorktown, Gettysburg, and Normandy. The veterans deserved better heirs.

It was also at West Point that I developed an academic association with Latin America. All cadets had to take a foreign language. The languages offered were German, French, Spanish, Arabic, Russian, Chinese, and Portuguese. Hundreds of cadets signed up for the first three. The next three were said to be supremely difficult because of the necessity of learning new and strange alphabets.

At an assembly near the end of basic training, the language departments presented their cases, looking for fresh meat. I was from a small town in Arkansas, and I feared getting lost in the crowd if I took

French, German, or Spanish. Furthermore, I had had Spanish in high school and found it boring—it also seemed a useless class to take in the middle of the Ozarks, at least when one figures with normal adolescent utilitarianism. As a plebe, I figured the last thing I would need was extra work, so that ruled out Arabic, Chinese, and Russian. When the Portuguese instructor made his pitch, I noticed that his overhead viewgraphs contained words very similar to Spanish words. He said Portuguese was the language to take, especially if any of us had a background in Spanish, and if we liked class sizes even smaller than average size at West Point. Class sizes at the Military Academy normally average less than fifteen. I had several Portuguese classes of three or four students and one class where I was the only student.

So, for reasons of freshman convenience, I chose Portuguese and proceeded to do quite well. In fact, when the time came to choose my "concentration"—the term used in those days at West Point to denote how we would spend the few electives allotted to us in the science-heavy curriculum—I chose Portuguese again. By the time I left the Academy, I had a firm grounding in Latin American studies.

Perhaps it was the odd combination of being a Portuguese-speaking West Point football player from Arkansas, but I won a Rhodes scholarship my senior year. When I graduated, I served a few months as a football coach and physical education instructor at the Military Academy Prep School at Fort Monmouth, New Jersey. In October of 1982, I left for Great Britain.

Oxford University afforded me a chance to deepen an interest in military and Latin American history. I was able to couple this with continued study of Portuguese. I visited Portugal four times, improving my language abilities by traveling and by attending a language school in Lisbon. However, the twenty-two months I spent at Oxford was time away from troops. My classmates were laboring as platoon leaders and company executive officers. In the summer of 1984, I returned to the Army, wiser, but behind. I had chosen the Corps of Engineers as a branch as a senior cadet—one of the original purposes of the Academy was to train engineer officers, and some of the greatest generals in our history began in the Corps—Lee, MacArthur, and Goodpaster among them. It seemed a wise choice.

After Engineer Officer Basic Course, I reported to the 15th Engineer Battalion (Combat) of the 9th Infantry Division (Motorized) for my first assignment as a platoon leader. The 15th was located at Fort Lewis, Washington, about 10 miles south of Tacoma and 45 miles south of Seattle. Fort Lewis was also the home of I Corps Headquarters (the First Corps, but everywhere pronounced "Eye" Corps). I Corps served as the peacetime higher headquarters for several active and reserve units in the Pacific Northwest.

The Army Engineers have two broad categories of battalions—combat and combat heavy. In the 1980s, the former were found organic to divisions (called divisional battalions) and at corps level (called corps combat). The divisional battalions were responsible for organizing the terrain of the battlefield for the division commander. In the defense, this generally meant erecting man-made obstacles or reinforcing natural obstacles through the emplacement of barbed wire, minefields, antitank ditches, and road craters. It also meant digging in vehicles and command posts. These missions were referred to as "countermobility" and "survivability." In the offense, engineers breached enemy obstacles; maintained, improved, or built roads and trails, and provided water-crossing capabilities, usually through construction of fording sites or bridges. This was called "mobility." The divisional battalions were limited in their construction capabilities, and most of what they built was expedient and intended to last only in the short term. The corps combat battalions had essentially the same mission and capabilities as the divisional battalion but had more construction capabilities. They were often pushed forward into the divisional area to reinforce the divisional battalions. With the right kind of equipment, both types of battalions were capable of building dirt airstrips for landing lighter aircraft. Divisional and corps combat battalions could also be reconfigured to fight as infantry when necessary. Because of that requirement, they were still all male.

The combat heavy battalions were also referred to as construction battalions. They had both horizontal- and vertical-construction platoons. Horizontal construction referred to the building of roads, airfields, and heliports. Vertical construction referred to the erecting of buildings and standing structures. These units were found at corps level and above. The construction specialists in these units were also trained in obstacle emplacement, bridging, and breaching to support divisional operations when necessary. Women were allowed to serve in construction units.

I reached the 15th Engineer Battalion in February 1985, five years after my experience with the 101st. Much had changed. President Reagan had been elected. With him came a return of patriotism, flag-waving, and respect for the military. The Army started a massive antidrug campaign through urinalysis. It became nearly impossible for an addict to avoid the test. When caught, the addicts or abusers were reformed or dismissed. With them went many of the other disciplinary problems. Resources again flowed to the services, and manning percentages went up.

My first platoon was a bridge between the two eras. My platoon sergeant had two years of college. He had made his rank, E7, in less than eleven years. He had a rapid intelligence and a cutting wit. The rest of the platoon and the soldiers were a mixture of the old and the new. Some of the NCOs were of the kind that had been available in 1980. So were some of the privates. Yet many of the younger soldiers and NCOs were quite intelligent. Several had been to college. By the time I left my platoon, most of the bad soldiers had left the Army, one way or another. Their replacements were almost all of high caliber. Unfortunately, the idea that the Army was a cash cow for college or an alternate votech and that barracks life should be as easy as possible to keep attracting volunteers persisted.

2
Assignment to Honduras

In November 1985, I had just been moved from one of the best jobs in the U.S. Army Corps of Engineers - that of combat engineer platoon leader - to one of the most ill-defined, brigade engineer. Platoon leaders command a small group of twenty to forty soldiers, living, training, and working in close proximity to the troops and NCOs. Platoons are at the heart of most Army operations. In the Engineers, combat platoons normally supported maneuvering armor or infantry battalions, accomplishing the countermobility, survivability, and mobility tasks required to enable the battalion to defend or attack. The job was physically and mentally demanding. Yet, many Engineer officers think the job the most psychologically rewarding of any an officer can hold.

The *concept* of brigade engineer was not a bad one. The officer functioned as the senior engineer staff officer and advisor to an armor or infantry brigade commander. Every division was composed of brigades, which the division commander maneuvered around the battlefield. Each brigade was composed of several battalions of armor and infantry. The number of armor or infantry battalions depended on the brigade mission, and shifted from mission to mission. The engineer staff officer was responsible for advising the commander on the desirability and feasibility of certain courses of action during combat operations. He was the brigade's point of contact for terrain analysis, obstacle emplacement, water-crossing support, and breaching support. The job involved coordinating the operations of all the engineer assets operating in the brigade's sector, coordinating with engineer headquarters adjacent to the brigade and with higher headquarters for additional support. The brigade engineer and his tiny staff tracked all obstacles, enemy and friendly, in the brigade's area, and all other engineer missions being carried out or already completed. This required much paper shuffling, the maintenance of map overlays, radio/telephone logs, minefield report forms, engineer reconnaissance reports, and the continual planning of future operations. The preferred method of planning involved the Engineer Estimate, which supported the Estimate-of-the-Situation process, which the entire brigade staff used to recommend courses of action to the brigade commander.

Unfortunately, the concept was not close to the reality. The brigade engineer in the 9th Infantry Division (referred to as "9th ID") was neither fish nor fowl. He was said to belong to the brigade with whom he worked, but in garrison, his office was miles away, at the divisional engineer battalion headquarters. The garrison job required going to weekly staff meetings at the brigade headquarters and little else for ten months out of the year. That left the brigade engineer open for any "shitty little job" available in the battalion. These would be performed under his additional duty as special projects officer (SPO). The other two months were spent in the field with the brigade on semiannual exercises.

In the field, the brigade engineer was worked nearly to death. The cell in the brigade main headquarters had to be manned twenty-four hours a day by someone competent enough to answer engineer-related questions, conduct the continuous planning, and operate the communications equipment. The position was authorized a major, a sergeant first class (E7), another sergeant (E5), and a driver. Most often, the cell had a captain or lieutenant, a staff sergeant (E6), and a driver, either a Specialist (E4) or a private. Unfortunately, it seemed that the sergeants and the drivers assigned to the sections were ones no one else wanted. Additionally, staff sergeants and lower ranking enlisted men did not have the experience or the staff training necessary to completely handle a full shift. For that matter, neither did many of the lieutenants and junior captains assigned to the job.

I was assigned there as a promotable first lieutenant, with two months until promotion. Even though I did not have much experience, especially as a staff officer, I thought I could do well enough on my first exercise, which was to be a TEAM SPIRIT deployment to Korea. Nonetheless, in the Army of the mid-1980s, one simple mistake could ruin a career, and the opportunity to fail was giving me some apprehension. Additionally, even though my staff sergeant and driver were competent enough, neither could be counted on to do the necessary staff work. They just didn't have the required training, and there was not enough time to train them, even if I had had the experience necessary to train them properly. The thought of returning from TEAM SPIRIT to spend several months twiddling my thumbs was also unappealing. Consequently, I was in the frame of mind to accept any other job that came along.

An additional concern was the commander of the brigade who understood much better than most the operations and roles of supporting branches, such as the engineers, signal units, and logisticians. What he did not know, he made a point to learn. His knowledge and exacting standards made it difficult for any but the best to serve him adequately. I thought I might be good enough, but I sure did not want to let him or the unit down in some crucial operation and then suffer the inevitable dressing-down that would follow. With this commander on the watch, the inexperienced, the untrained, and the inept had no place to hide. I looked forward to learning from the man, but two months out of the year were not enough, and the cost of any mistake was very high.

I first heard about the Honduran engineer job through the grapevine. I also heard that it would be offered to the one engineer captain in the 15th who was not in direct line to command the first available engineer company—the captain whose shoes I had just filled at brigade engineer. I called this officer and asked him if he planned to take the job. His answer was negative. He did not want to lose any chance to command that might come up. I next called the 15th's adjutant and scheduled a conference with the battalion commander.

My plan was to volunteer. The Honduran job called for a captain, and I would be one in a few weeks. I had practically no knowledge of the job requirements, although I did know a fair amount about the country and the region from my college studies—mainly that it was dirt-poor, horribly underdeveloped, and sandwiched between the Marxist guerrillas of El Salvador and the Marxist Sandinistas of Nicaragua. I did not even know the exact tour length. But sometimes the devil you don't know is better than the devil you do.

The battalion commander accepted my offer to go. However, he said that he would first try to get released from the commitment; he did not want to lose an officer for six months. Neither did the only other engineer unit at Fort Lewis, a construction battalion assigned to I Corps.

But the I Corps battalion already had an officer detailed to Southern Command (SOUTHCOM) in Panama for six months so my battalion was stuck with the tasking, and by Thanksgiving, I knew I was going.

Even though the primary reason for my going was to get out of the brigade engineer job, I was not totally unfamiliar with our actions in Central America ("CENTAM" in Army-speak). I had been reading about our operations there and the seemingly inevitable political controversy that accompanied them. Military engineering was a large part of the effort. I had studied the history of Latin America at the Academy and after. I also completely supported the idea of helping strengthen Central America, particularly the country of Honduras, which faced the dual threat of the communist Frente Farabundo Marti de la Liberacion National (FMLN) in El Salvador, and the communist Frente Sandinista de Liberacion Nacional (FSLN) that controlled Nicaragua.[3] I was excited and proud that I was going to be a part of what we were doing.

But getting there involved a bureaucratic maze typical of the Army. A serviceman can go nowhere without written orders. I arranged to pick mine up by 3 December 1985, a month and three days before my departure. Also on 3 December, I arranged to get a new set of prescription glasses and made my travel arrangements. A terrorism briefing was next on 4 December.

The terrorism briefing consisted of a civilian employee handing me a sheaf of documents and telling me to ask if I had any questions. He also gave me a little wallet card containing tips to lessen my exposure to possible terrorism ("Avoid revealing your plans; avoid routine schedules; keep a low profile; avoid going out alone"). Naturally, I had to sign my name to indicate that I had been to the "briefing" and had been trained on countering the terrorist threat. No wonder that we were vulnerable to losing servicemen overseas to bombings and shootings in this period.

After the briefing, I drew an issue of jungle gear: four sets of lightweight fatigues, two sets of jungle boots, mosquito netting, two-quart canteen, and two floppy bush hats. I mailed copies of my orders and flight data to Honduras on 5 December. On 6 December, our battalion intelligence section (the S2) fingerprinted me for easier identification of my body in case of death, a standard procedure. I turned in my officer rating support form on 12 December. On 16 December, I opened a new bank account with a monthly allotment to keep my finances separate from those of my wife, a necessity in the time before digital, on-line banking. The same day, I had the tailors add twenty-seven dollar's worth of patches and insignia to my jungle uniforms. The next day, I got all but one of the requisite tropical immunizations at a troop medical clinic in the morning. That afternoon the dental clinic began two days of work, including panographic X rays, also to be used in case of my death. On 19 December, the Army issued me an airline ticket with an open return date. I mailed copies of the panographic X rays and fingerprint cards to Honduras on the same day. On 27 December 1985, I picked up $1,755 from the finance office in advanced temporary duty pay to defray expenses. I also signed up for family-separation allowance—two dollars per day, the value the government had established as compensation for the geographical splitting of families. My final stop was to get a nuclear, biological, and chemical (NBC) protective mask to take with me in my baggage. Nobody really expected the Sandinistas or any of the other unsavory elements in the region to use poison gas or biological weapons, but with the world the way it was, being prepared was best. In any case, a protective mask also served as a good makeshift pillow.

With the orders came more information on my job, phone numbers, and points of contact. The organization to which I would be assigned was Joint Task Force-Bravo (JTFB) based at Palmerola Air Base (PAB), Honduras. The mission of the task force was support for the periodic exercises run by U.S. forces in Honduras, something called "continuing presence." My particular job was not described well, but was in the joint task force engineer office. My orders merely said "Augmentation for U.S. Mil in Honduras" and "Travel for Training." This was my first exposure to the bureaucratically obfuscating use of the word "training."

I called the Honduran number given to me by the Fort Lewis and I Corps tasking office to ascertain any specifics I could about my job. I spoke with an Air Force captain and Army lieutenant, both of whom told similar stories. The office was undermanned, but running well. They desperately needed engineering books and manuals. The work centered on keeping the air base functional, as well as planning and executing support for deploying exercise units. Both confirmed the need for the jungle equipment and described the living conditions as primitive—the billets were something called CAT huts, a variation of SEA huts. I was later to learn that the acronyms stood for Central American Tropical hut and Southeast Asian huts.

I was to discover later that these accommodations were kept relatively primitive because of the intended temporary nature of the U.S. facility. To my surprise, they said that most of the huts had TVs and refrigerators.

In view of the need for manuals, I ransacked the battalion's library and borrowed other construction manuals from a captain who had already completed the Engineer Officers Advanced Course, where construction techniques and processes were taught. As I had not yet attended the Advanced Course, I was not well grounded in drainage, vertical and horizontal construction, and the important planning concepts that the job implied. I spent most of December reading the manuals I had borrowed.

I also read as much as I could find on the country of Honduras and our current role there. In the years afterward and before writing the original edition, I added to this initial research in order to better understand what we were doing in Honduras and my role in it. What follows here should give the casual reader enough background and doctrinal information to correctly place our 1986 operations in the web of history.

3
THE COUNTRY

Honduras is a country about the size of the state of Ohio. The population in 1986 was approximately 4.3 million with an annual growth rate of 3.5 percent. The capital, Tegucigalpa, had a population of 360,000. The second largest city, San Pedro Sula, had 160,000. Honduras had few roads, and of those, less than 2000 kilometers (1200 miles) were paved. Less than 1200 kilometers (720 miles) of railway were still operational, the bulk of which served the banana regions of the Caribbean coast. Puerto Cortes and Puerto Castilla on the Caribbean and San Lorenzo on the Pacific were the only major port facilities in 1986. Major airports were located at Tegucigalpa, San Pedro Sula, Goloson, and at Palmerola.

Honduras is a land of contrasts. The Caribbean coast is extremely wet and tropical. In the center and in the south, the climate is more temperate, with large pine forests. The center and south also experience a very dry season from December through May, followed by a very wet season. Valley floors and coastal plains suffer under blistering heat, but mountainous slopes and ridges are cool, verging on cold.

These contrasts are also true in the social and economic spheres. Honduras was the Central American country with the best land distribution among the peasants. Honduras also had the most organized labor force in Central America, a legacy from the highly developed fruit industry. On the other hand, per capita, Honduras was the poorest non-island nation in the Americas. Yet, because of land distribution and the agricultural economy, many of the people grew what they ate, and ate relatively well, despite having very little disposable income.[4]

The history of Honduras is not a pretty one. It was a backwater of the Spanish Empire in America. When independence movements broke out in the Spanish colonies during and after the Napoleonic Wars, Honduras and its Central American neighbors lagged behind the rest. Like so much else in Honduran history, events outside the region were the proximate cause for actions at home.

In 1820, Mexico, under Agustin de Iturbide, declared itself independent of Spain. In 1822, de Iturbide proclaimed himself emperor and asked the Central American provinces to join him.[5] These provinces had suffered during the Napoleonic era as the wars and political disruptions collapsed the European markets for Central American agricultural goods. Spanish mercantilist policies prohibited the colonies from legally trading with other nations. Not surprisingly, the Honduran farmers and merchants, and their counterparts in the other provinces, desired economic freedom and legal access to other markets.

The Central American provinces were hardly unified political entities. Rather, each was a loose collection of towns. Often, the major towns rarely had much to do with one another. Communication relied on very rough tracks snaking over the high mountains or through the jungle. The inevitable result was government by local strongmen—*caudillos,* or *generales.* In 1874, the U.S. ambassador to Guatemala succinctly described the major factors preventing Central American unity. Among the most important were "local prejudices, a heterogeneous population, lack of a common interest, difficulty of intercommunication, and a lack of a prominent leader."[6] This description could serve equally well for conditions in 1574, and perhaps even as late as 1974, and although the description addressed Central American unity then, it is a sufficient explanation for the lack of internal unity within any of the current Central American states in the 1980s.

Yet Central America did experience a brief period of unity. When his offer of annexation was ignored, de Iturbide threatened to send Mexican troops to force the Central Americas to join his "empire." Fighting broke out in the provinces between those who favored the Mexican offer and those opposed. The latter group dominated. Faced with the threat from Mexico and the desire for economic freedom, the leaders of the provinces jointly declared their independence from Spain as the "United Provinces of the Center of America" on July 1, 1823.[7]

The brief unity of Central America, spawned by the threats from Mexico and Spain, centered on Francisco Morazán, a liberal general born in Tegucigalpa.[8] He fought twenty-one battles between 1827 and 1840 in the cause of the Union, ultimately failing. The fact that efforts at unity required so much internecine fighting says a great deal about Central

America, then and now. By 1839, only the rump of the Union, centered in El Salvador, remained to Morazán and his forces. Honduras, Costa Rica, Nicaragua, and most of Guatemala had gone their own ways. Nonetheless, Morazán remains a hero to most people in the region, especially to those of his birthplace.[9]

Indeed, the concept of unity or of Central American "otherness" still endures. The flag of Honduras has five stars, each representing the states of the former Union. Also, Honduran products are usually stamped with "Honduras, C.A.," the initials representing "Central America," in much the same way Americans write "Little Rock, AR., USA." The reality of unity, though, is no closer now than it was in 1823. What unity there is among the nations is still often prompted by threats from the outside.

HISTORY OF U.S. INVOLVEMENT IN CENTRAL AMERICA (CENTAM)

Strategically, Honduras is geographical and political key terrain in Central America. Its borders touch Guatemala, El Salvador, Nicaragua, the Caribbean, and the Pacific. Consequently, Honduras's position dominates the Isthmus of Panama.

Countries do not often escape their geographies. Since it became heavily dependent on maritime trade in the later Middle Ages, Britain has had to be concerned with who controlled the ports of the Low Countries. Even after the world shifted from a Mediterranean-centered economy to an Atlantic-centered economy in the sixteenth century, the Low Countries themselves, by virtue of their geography, have generally contained the largest ports in Europe and the world in terms of volume. Similarly, a united Germany in the middle of Europe had to be concerned with foreign powers to its east and west. Conversely, America, with weak neighbors to north and south, was able to grow in relative isolation until the middle of the twentieth century and the advent of fast navies, long-range bombers, and missiles. Indeed, one of America's enduring concerns has been the extension of the power of a foreign country into the New World. Even in the modern world where technology has mitigated much of the isolation that geography once afforded some countries, any such extension of foreign power and influence into the Americas would still have enormous strategic implications. America is as much a prisoner of geography as any other country.

International relations theorists have noted that patterns recur endlessly in the affairs among nations. The geographical influences cited above are examples of such patterns.[10] A very quick review of U.S. involvement in Central America can serve to reinforce this notion.

Worried about a resurgence of European colonialism in the New World in the wake of Napoleon's defeat, President Monroe proclaimed his famous doctrine in December of 1823 only a few months after the Central American Union had declared its independence from Spain. That worry has continued until this very day. Some respected academics maintain that there has never been a real threat to the United States.[11] Hence, to them, the Monroe Doctrine has merely served as a convenient pre-text for the extension of American hegemony over the entire hemisphere generally, and of the Caribbean Basin in particular. Yet, a review of the international events since 1823 certainly gives the impression that outside powers did indeed seek to extend their influence. As the section on geography above shows, the United States could not be indifferent to such moves.

The case of William Walker in the 1850s represents to many an early manifestation of American imperialism. Throughout the 1840s, British and American interests had contended over the issue of transit across the Central American isthmus. These interests saw Panama and Nicaragua as possible sites for a future canal.[12] Until such a canal could be built, shipping and rail companies provided the necessary transit from the Caribbean to the Pacific. Walker's episode was an outgrowth of this competition.

Indeed, to one scholar, Walker was nothing more than a "front man for the U.S. financial interests that exerted strong influence over U.S. foreign policy."[13] While lending no credibility to this conspiracy-theory assertion, certain American financiers acting in concert with Nicaraguan liberals did, indeed, back the Walker expedition. In 1855, Walker landed in Nicaragua with slightly over fifty men. With this paltry force, he was able to conquer the country. Moreover, he received American recognition according to the international customs of the time. It is this official recognition of Walker that causes many to see a quasi-official link between Walker and the U.S. government.

By conquering Nicaragua, however, Walker angered Cornelius Vanderbilt who had steamship and rail interests in the area. He also angered the British. The British and Vanderbilt collaborated to raise and arm a Central American army in Costa Rica to liberate Nicaragua, which was done in May 1857. Walker would make three subsequent attempts to reconquer Nicaragua. The first two were frustrated by American warships—a strange action by an imperial-minded power. Walker's third attempt was his last. He landed again in 1860, this time in Honduras, only to be promptly captured by British troops. They turned him over to the Honduran authorities who then executed him.[14] Hence, the pattern of transitory Central American cooperation and unity, brought on always by the interventions and threats of outside forces, is well established. Equally well established is the intervention of outsiders—in Walker's case, the Americans and the British acting on behalf of the Central Americans.

Also in the late 1850s, Mexico was rife with political unrest between the anti-clerical liberals and the pro-church conservatives. As a result, Mexico went into arrears in debt payments to the British, French, and Spanish. In December 1860, with the United States on the brink of civil war due to the election of Abraham Lincoln just the month before, the three European nations sent a joint expeditionary force to Mexico to seize the Mexican customs houses at Vera Cruz and pay themselves the money Mexico owed from taxes imposed on imports and exports passing through the port.

The French, though, under Napoleon III, were interested in far more than debt payments. They sought the conquest of Mexico. When this plan became apparent to the British and the Spanish, they withdrew. The French would remain until February 1867, establishing Maximilian, an archduke from the Austrian royal family, as a puppet emperor.

There is some evidence that Napoleon III was quite anti-American. His feelings flowed from the attachment he had to the romantic vision of monarchical rule. Hence, he could barely abide the republican example set by the United States, even as this country suffered through its civil war. The Mexican adventure seemed a prime opportunity to reestablish monarchical rule in the republican areas of Latin America.

Napoleon Ill's chosen instrument, Maximilian, was himself a dreamer, an Austrian prince who was a favorite of the French court. His wife, a Belgian princess, was a friend of Queen Victoria. Maximilian saw himself creating a great Latin American empire linked to the royal houses of Europe. He even entertained the notion of arranging the marriage of his younger brother to the Princess Isabella of Brazil, a member of the Portuguese royal house. In this way, Maximilian could create an enormous Latin Empire in the New World, composed of Mexico in the north and Brazil in the south.[15]

In pursuit of their dream, the French deployed over forty thousand troops to Mexico, and these were reinforced by several thousand more Austrians and Belgians. Although Mexican resistance did much to thwart Napoleon's plans, it was the deployment under General Sheridan of fifty thousand veteran Union troops along the Rio Grande, coupled with direct U.S. demands for withdrawal that convinced the French to leave. Once its internal affairs were settled, the U.S. acted forcefully to eliminate a perceived threat on its borders, a threat created by an outside power.

By the end of the French intervention, a clear pattern of U.S. concerns had emerged. First and foremost, the United States feared instability in the region closest to its southern borders. Why? Because such instability provided the opportunities and pretext for meddling by outside powers. Consequently, the United States viewed the actions of Walker with a jaundiced eye because of his potential to create chaos that might redound to the favor of the British. The instability of Mexico that brought on the French intervention could only have confirmed such views. Other crises at the turn of the nineteenth century and shortly thereafter exacerbated this fear of intervention by the other great powers.

In 1895 and again in 1902, Britain and Germany threatened Venezuela over territorial and debt disputes. In 1904, Germany made threatening moves toward the Dominican Republic. Fueling these crises was the growing naval competition between Britain and Germany. Navies of that era needed numerous coaling stations. If Germany sought to be a credible naval power, it, too, needed overseas bases. If it could gain them in the Caribbean, it might also turn a strategic flank of the British. Mahan's naval theory that truly great nations were also great sea powers lent further credence to these views.

The United States viewed the extension of European quarrels into American waters with alarm. America had recently ejected from the Caribbean the Spanish, whose colonial rule had become increasingly feeble and ruthless, and by so doing became responsible for Cuba and Puerto Rico. The Roosevelt corollary to the Monroe Doctrine and the institution of dollar diplomacy were direct results of this alarm. American capital and American might would be the instruments to secure the Caribbean basin from instabilities induced by debts to the Europeans, or from the grand designs of European statesmen.[16]

In the second decade of the twentieth century, America's interventions became numerous as the events in Europe and Central America simultaneously worsened.[17] There were interventions in Haiti, Nicaragua, and Mexico. In the first two, the questions were again debt and challenges to the ruling parties, and the fears of European opportunism. In Mexico, as happened in the 1850s and 1860s, fighting broke out among the various classes, leaders, factions, and regions. The United States, over a matter of principle, intervened directly at Vera Cruz in 1914, using thousands of Marines and soldiers. Barely two years later, Army troops under General Pershing spent months chasing Pancho Villa because our southern border had become unsafe because of the revolution.

Other questions wrapped up in the web of international events of those turbulent, bloody years involved the belligerents in the war then going on in Europe. Mexico had significant oil and mineral holdings. Would the revolution cut those supplies off from the growing U.S. economy? Would the European powers attempt to secure those supplies solely for themselves by backing one Mexican faction over another? Since President Wilson was avowedly pro-British, would the Central Powers attempt to woo Mexico to counter any American intervention in Europe? The answer to the last question came with the Zimmerman telegram.

In January 1917, Germany came to the conclusion that it needed to adopt unrestricted submarine warfare. Since war with the United States was a likely result, the Germans sought to establish a German-Japanese-Mexican alliance to contain America. On 19 January 1917, the German foreign secretary, Alfred Zimmerman, sent a coded message to his ambassador in Mexico. The message proposed an alliance with Mexico, and suggested that war might bring back to Mexico territories that it had lost in the Mexican-American war seventy years before. The British intercepted the message and turned it over, gleefully no doubt, to the American government. The State Department released the decoded message to the media on 1 March 1917, causing widespread public outcries against the Germans. Barely a month later, the United States declared war.

American interventions continued after World War I until 1933. The advent of President Franklin Roosevelt, the Depression, and the fascist threat brought a curious sort of peace and unity to the Americas that lasted until the 1950s. Then, the latest threat to the Americas appeared in earnest—the ideological threat of communism, backed by the resources of the Soviet Union. Many of the episodes in this arena of the Cold War are quite familiar to students of recent history. The United States successfully supported the toppling of the left-leaning Arbenz government in Guatemala in 1954, yet finished the decade by losing Cuba. In the 1960s and 1970s, we lent doctrinal and material support to many efforts. Che Guevarra was tracked down and killed in the Bolivian mountains. The Brazilians, Argentinians, and Uruguayans fought communist-led urban insurgencies. Other rebellions continued to simmer in Guatemala, Nicaragua, Columbia, and Peru. The cost of fighting the latest threat was high - some critics would say too high—in terms of lives, money, material, and stunted democracy. Nevertheless, with the total victory of the West in the Cold War, all Latin American and Caribbean countries adopted some form of democratic government by the mid-1990s, except for the aging and decaying dictatorship in Cuba. Even after the Cold War, the U.S. and allies intervened in Haiti in 1994 to topple the Cedras dictatorship, and again in 2004 to restore order when the Haitian government collapsed.

American governments may originally have become involved in Latin America because of the threat of European imperialism. This may have changed to a more direct concern with our physical security, in the first instance during the pre-World War I and pre-World War II years, and again since the 1950s. Throughout, though, there had also been idealism involved: against colonialism, imperialism, fascism, or communism; for democracy and liberal notions of freedom. Radical theorists might dismiss any or all of these motivations and maintain that all American activities derived from the desire to protect American investments, businesses, and properties. Yet Americans had so few interests in so many of the small countries that this cannot be a compelling argument. In the end, the pattern has continued: America intervenes to protect its national security and to maintain the power that it currently has. These were the basic notions behind the Reagan Doctrine, as they were behind the Monroe Doctrine. However, "power" and "security" are defined in different ways in different ages.

As stated near the beginning, patterns recur endlessly in the affairs among nations. In the 1980s, the pattern reestablished itself when America once again faced a direct threat from a non-hemispheric power.

THE 1980s: INSTABILITY, EXERCISES, AND CONTINUING PRESENCE

In 1979, instability broke out in the Caribbean once more. Marxist governments came to power in Grenada and Nicaragua. In El Salvador, several communist groups went into open rebellion. In Nicaragua, the Sandinistas overthrew the unpopular Somoza regime. As the Sandinistas drifted ever leftward, it became apparent that the El Salvadoran insurgency was receiving open help from the Nicaraguans and their newfound benefactors, the Cubans and the Soviets. The Sandinistas proclaimed theirs to be a revolution without borders. In tiny Grenada, the New Jewel movement eagerly invited the Soviets and Cubans to use their island. In the middle of all of this was Honduras, itself still ruled by a military dictatorship. Refugees from both El Salvador and Nicaragua flocked to Honduras to flee the fighting, exacerbating already dire economic conditions.[18]

By 1981, it was obvious to all except the most committed that the Sandinistas had no intention of establishing a true democracy in Nicaragua. Furthermore, arms shipments were flowing quite freely to the El Salvadoran FMLN. The El Salvadoran rebel leaders met openly in Managua. On Grenada, Cubans began constructing an airfield out of all proportion to the kind needed to support tourism. Groups of former Somoza guardsmen, Miskito Indians, and the generally disaffected began armed operations against the Sandinistas from Honduran soil. They were quickly supported by the new Reagan administration. In October 1983, the United States and its regional allies in the eastern Caribbean took advantage of an attempted coup on Grenada to restore order and rid the place of Cubans and Soviets. Also in 1983, the United States began a series of military exercises in Honduras.

Militarily, the Honduran Air Force was the largest and best

equipped in Central America, even though the bulk of its planes were of Korean War vintage. The attitude of the Honduran military had been anticommunist, if not totally pro-American. Recognizing the threat growing around it, the Honduran military conducted several operations against the El Salvadoran guerrillas along El Salvador's southern border from 1980 to 1983, some in conjunction with the government forces of their traditional rival, El Salvador. Yet, faced with conflict on two sides, the traditionally small Honduran military, mostly a conscript force, was hard pressed.

As the Sandinista threat grew, the main focus of the Honduran military shifted eastward. Skirmishing broke out along the eastern border several times from 1983 on. In 1983 and again in 1984, the Honduran military intercepted columns of leftist guerrillas in the eastern districts of the country. These guerrillas had been trained and outfitted in Nicaragua and Cuba. In the same period, the anti-Sandinista Contra movement gained enough adherents and U.S. aid to become a credible force. The Nicaraguan Contras sought sanctuary on Honduran soil along the Rio Coco, the ill-defined boundary between the two nations.

Beginning in1983, the U.S. and Honduran armed forces conducted a series of joint and combined exercises in Honduras to strengthen that country and to show U.S. resolve in the face of the growing threats. Two early-warning radar facilities were built. In conjunction with the government of Honduras, Palmerola Airfield was upgraded to handle all types of cargo planes, and Goloson Airfield in La Ceiba was slated for similar upgrade. A regional military training center was established at Trujillo, Honduras, to train the expanding El Salvadoran and Honduran armies. Five dirt strips were constructed or upgraded to allow C-130 landings. Combat troops from all the services participated in each of these exercises.[19] [See Appendix C for a list of major exercises conducted 1983-86.]

Incidental to the pure military infrastructure operations, the U.S. military, primarily engineers and medical personnel, conducted many civic-action programs. Wells were drilled; roads were improved; schools were constructed or upgraded. During operation AHUAS TARA II, conducted in late 1983 and early 1984, over fifty-four thousand medical and dental patients were treated, and more than two hundred thousand people inoculated (5 percent of the total Honduran population). Equally important to an agricultural country, military veterinarians treated thousands of head of peasants' livestock.

It was into this setting that I was heading. I was promoted to captain on 31 December 1985. On 6 January, I left for Honduras.

4
PALMEROLA AIR BASE

In reply to a bit of left wing drivel the magazine had seen fit to publish on the subject of the immorality of America's Central American policies, I sent a letter to the editor of the *American Oxonian*. I told the editor that I was about to be "posted to Honduras for six months to take a direct part in the Reagan administration's Central American policy, for good or ill, as history will ultimately tell us."

> The core of the arguments over our foreign policy [in Central America] is how best to apply JFK's belief that America should "pay any price, bear any burden, meet any hardship, fight any foe, to assure the survival and success of liberty." To do that, whether the case is Poland, Afghanistan, Angola, or Nicaragua, means we must define what we mean by "liberty," "friend," and "foe," and if America will, in fact, bear any sacrifices at all for such goals, and if so, how much sacrifice.
>
> *The American Oxonian,* Spring 1986, Volume LXXIII, Number 2, 144-45

DIARY

6 Jan 1986, 1900 hours, Fort Lewis, Washington
Waiting for Captain H to arrive to take me to the airport. Loneliness is already setting in.

I'm kind of excited. Not the least because I'm traveling through two major airports—SEA-TAC here in Granola Land, and Miami in Sun & Fun Land. My countrymen are continually fascinating to me. Their pretensions, fads, self-security, diversity, affluence are still baffling and wondrous.

Of course, the country and region I'm going to also fascinate me. The truths or myths I might find are scary. However, I go armed with better knowledge of the history of the region and our involvement in it than the bulk of those serving there.

What are my goals? Aside from doing the job (of which I still know very little), I want to contribute to the Honduran society in some way—drainage, sewerage, or wells. I want to help educate my colleagues about our role in Central America, about my perceptions of our proper, reduced role in the world, about our need to stand up for ourselves . . .

2355 hours, 6 January 1986 SEA-TAC International
Boarding takes place in thirty-five minutes. I'm in SEA-TAC's USO lounge. So many young faces around. On TV, Ed Luttwak and General Meyer are debating the possible courses of action open to Libya and the United States with respect to the recent terrorist attacks and our possible retaliation. Luttwak is afraid that Libya would attack U.S. bases in Sicily, driving a wedge between us and our wavering allies (I'm tempted to call them leeches).

7 January 1986, 1150 hours EST, Miami International
Sitting in the middle of Crockett and Tubbs Land. This is the only U.S. airport I've been in that remotely approaches the cosmopolitanism of the major European airports. The two most common languages are Spanish and English, but the lilt of the Caribbean islanders is here too. A Pan Am flight just arrived from Hamburg, Germany. Those speaking the languages are of all colors.

The two currencies most noticeable are money (of any and all kinds) and freedom. The citizens of our southern neighbors sitting around me definitely are not beggars. The women are too slim, too glamorous, the men too elegant. The odd American, myself included, stands out because of our generally plain dress ("tasteless" according to my Portuguese tutors in Lisbon). These Caribbean and Latin American elites flock here because of the fun, the opportunity, and the security. Comforting this ardent nationalist is that they all appear to have a command of English—no doubt useful should they have to follow their money here when, or if, their countries fall.

This melting pot must approach old New York City, and certainly that of modern Los Angeles. However, I much prefer what seems to be the respect for America evident among the people here. It is only a feeling, but the cousins of these travelers who have made Florida their new home indicate that immigrants from these regions can assimilate as readily as the Europeans before them. The anti-gringo attitudes of certain immigrant groups, legal or not, bothers me.

The Americans are dressed in corduroys or jeans, and tennis shoes. Most male foreigners are dressed in slacks, button-down shirts, and pointed leather shoes. The women prefer short dresses, and high heels with pointed toes.

On the same flight as mine, I can see a Honduran couple checking in far more than their two allowed forty-four-pound bags. Included is a complete Commodore computer and several other large boxes—also a large bag of disposable diapers.

8 January 1986, 0710 hours, Palmerola Air Base, Honduras
Got here last night at about 2000 hrs. Slept most of the way. We stopped to eat at the American embassy—quite fortress like. Completely puts to shame the old Lisbon embassy.

The scenery from the plane was beautiful—everything is so green. San Pedro Sula looked like, and is, a small city, but well kept and orderly. The mountains rise up quickly, confining living and working to the valley floors.

As we flew into Tegucigalpa, one could definitely see that this was not a wealthy or well-kept city. However, it did not appear to have suffered from the rampant slum building seen elsewhere in Latin America. The streets were straight and blocked. None of the houses were large, but what must be the middle-class dwellings were largely made of cinder block, with low roofs, often of sheet metal. In the immediate vicinity of the airport, the poverty was worse. The houses were wooden shacks. Also, the poor seemed to congregate at the airport. The people had all gone to the second floor to swamp the small balcony there to watch the planes come in. Some were so daring as to climb over the railing to stand, sit, or squat on the overhanging roof below.

Now for the good part. My luggage did not arrive. I gambled and lost by not even putting my shaving kit into my flight bag, nor any gym clothes. My flight bag is filled with field manuals and programmed texts, which will no doubt prove mighty useful in the job but do nothing for my immediate survival. If the bags do not arrive today, I'll be so smelly that I'll be forced to beg clothes.

The base looks very much like a boy's camp. To many here, it reminds them of base camps and firebases in Vietnam. The hootches are about three feet off the ground, have wooden floors, and screens covered by shutters for walls. The showers are sixteen-feet-by-thirty-two-feet GP Medium tents, stretched over wooden floors and frames. Little sidewalks run everywhere. Their construction consists of bricks placed in between two-by-sixes held up by stakes. Quite an orderly little village upon first impression-better in many respects than what the majority of the population has—some running water, a few flush toilets, electricity, and satellite TV dishes. However, I was impressed by how much electricity the country has—evidenced by the skylines I saw on last night's drive.

* * *

On the ride down from Miami, I sat next to an interesting man. I do not remember his occupation, but he was a member of a large contingent from Long Island that was heading to Belize for scuba diving. There must have been at least twenty of the divers on the small jet. He was just the first of many tourists I would bump into. None of them ever seemed concerned about war.

Upon landing at Belize City, I noticed immediately that the airport was surrounded by some of the latest anti-air systems of a strange design. Then I saw the Harrier aircraft parked in open revetments covered by camouflage netting, and understood. The advanced weapons belonged to the contingent of British troops that still garrison this former outpost of the empire (formerly called British Honduras). In addition to the air defense systems and the squadron of fighters, the Brits had an infantry battalion stationed here. Their numbers made them the second largest foreign military force in Central America north of the Canal. They were second only to the several thousand Cubans, Russians, and East Germans that were showing international socialist solidarity with the brave Sandinistas. The American forces at Palmerola ranked a mere third, but caused the most bellyaching in the legislatures and media of the Free World.

As I got off the airplane in Tegucigalpa, I wondered how I was ever going to get to Palmerola. The engineer office there had said that someone would be waiting for me. How I was to tell who it was in the mass of humanity gathered in the airport debarkation area was beyond me.

However, North Americans and Europeans were quite noticeable by their size. As I processed through immigration, an American of medium height, sunburned, balding approached to ask if I was Captain Waddell. He led me over to where baggage was off-loaded. Waiting there was a rather rough looking character, introduced to me as Sergeant First Class C.

When my baggage failed to show, my contact said not to worry, and took the Sergeant First Class and me through crowds of swarming, begging children to a Chevrolet three-quarter-ton pickup. All of the children wanted to carry our bags, wash our truck, or just guard our belongings. The sun was near setting as we piled in. The man who picked me up explained that he was a USAF Technical Sergeant (E6) from the engineer office at Palmerola. Sergeant First Class C. was his replacement and had come in on an earlier flight. The Tech Sergeant himself was due to leave in two days. With that information, we left for the American embassy, where, the Tech Sergeant informed us, we could get the most realistic American food in Honduras. Everyone from Palmerola, he said, made a point to eat there whenever they got a chance to come to the capital.

By the time we'd eaten hamburgers and ice cream, dark had fallen. The advance packet of information from JTFB had stated that U.S. personnel were forbidden to drive after dark. I asked the USAF sergeant what we would do. He agreed that it was prohibited but that no one paid much attention to the rule. Besides, we didn't have accommodations for the night, and we were expected back. In fact, many people stayed as long as they could in Tegucigalpa, and then dashed back to the base trying to beat the curfew. Failure was often, he said, and rarely punished. I was overly tired, without much cash, without clothes, and in no mood to seek rooms in a Third World capital at night. I didn't argue the point.

30

11 January 1986, PAB

What a hectic four days! Besides being to Comayagua twice and Tegucigalpa once, I've been trying to learn the job. The setup here at Palmerola is really fascinating. A regular temporary city getting more and more permanent.

Upon our arrival at Palmerola, the JTFB first sergeant issued me some sheets and took me to the transient hootch to find a bunk. The next morning I borrowed a towel and a razor from another transient and headed to the shower. People kept staring at me. I was fully clothed in corduroys, a polo shirt and leather loafers. Everyone else wore shorts and shower shoes.

After showering, I began my in-processing. The task force personnel office had me fill out several forms and sent me on my way to the weekly preventive-medicine briefing for newcomers. The briefing was held in a GP Medium tent in the sweltering tropical heat. The canvas seemed only to stifle any hope of a cool breeze. As the crowd entered the tent in twos and threes, the temperature rose even further. We all began to sweat. I was apparently the only person whose baggage had not arrived.

A female private first class (E3), who was no older than nineteen, gave the briefing to the largely male audience. She gleefully talked about the various maladies associated with service at Palmerola. She kept emphasizing personal choices and responsibilities.

"There's no approved place to eat down in Comayagua," she told us. "But if you just have to eat down there, don't worry. Come see us at the hospital when you get dysentery. There's also no approved dairy source in Honduras. Now, I wouldn't buy any of that ice cream they sell in the mall downtown, but some people just have to. That's all right. Just come on by when you get sick."

She continued in the same vein, as I marveled that a little out-of-the-way place like the nearby town of Comayagua had a mall. The private used the same tone when describing the sexually transmitted diseases that one could pick up from the local prostitutes.

"Some guys just have to fool around with those little Hondo girls down in the village. But that's okay, too. When you're done, just come on by, and we'll give you a dose of penicillin. Oh, by the way, eight of the local prostitutes have checked positive for AIDS. If any of you all get that, well, we *can't* help you at all. You just gotta understand the risks you're taking."

Surprisingly, the hospital ran a free check on the prostitutes every Thursday. Each woman was issued a book in which the American doctor would stamp his name if she checked out healthy. However, the young private told us that rumor had it the women had found a way to duplicate the stamps used, so the best policy was to leave the women alone. "But if you just have to indulge, then come on by the hospital ..." were her final remarks.

After changing most of my dollars into Honduran lempira at the finance hootch, I made it to the engineer office. The Sergeant First Class and the Air Force Technical Sergeant, my companions from the previous night, were already there. The person apparently in charge was an Army First Lieutenant. Another sergeant and a female Army specialist were typing away—obviously the clerks. Mounds of paperwork covered the two desks in the office. The Lieutenant was seated behind one of the desks, peering out over the piles. There were wooden counters built along one side of the hootch. These served as desks, and they were inundated in paper, too.

The Lieutenant explained the workings of the office as rapidly as the ringing phones permitted. The office was authorized four officers, two clerks, and five NCOs. The people present in the office were those available for work, but the Technical Sergeant was leaving in a couple of days. The Lieutenant also informed me that in three days, he was leaving on a three-day temporary-duty (TDY) trip to Atlanta, and the office would be mine. So much for an easy break-in period. I immediately set to work learning the job.

As I was about to die from the heat, the Lieutenant loaned me a pair of shorts, his shower shoes, and a West Point Twelfth Man T-shirt. I passed another night in the transient hootch, and on the morning of 9 January, I moved into hootch A35, and a bunk next to the Lieutenant's. I worked all day on the ninth in the borrowed outfit—which elicited looks of curiosity rather than surprise. On the tenth, my luggage and clean underwear finally arrived.

The grapevine had it that the Honduran national airline, Tan-Sahsa, gave first preference to the bags of Honduran citizens. This was not an unreasonable policy, but as my observation in the Miami airport had confirmed, few of these nationals ever returned with a standard load of luggage. Bags displaced by this civilian luggage usually followed on the first available flight, which might be routed through any number of Central American cities. Consequently, the bags of American GIs often arrived only after considerable delay.

One consequence of these delays was that they gave time for thieves to ransack the baggage. The USAF engineer captain in the office lost a portable stereo in this manner. He had packed it in his footlocker, which was delayed.

Other stories circulated about weapons being lost in a similar manner. The instructions assigning soldiers to PAB were sufficiently vague that some traveled with their assigned weapons. Some young GI might obtain authorization from the airlines, then break his weapon down and store it in his baggage. Naturally, the baggage would be delayed. Of course, the disassembled weapon would be gone. The stories usually had the baggage arriving in Honduras on a flight that had passed through Managua or San Salvador. Presumably, the weapons were stolen while in transit through one of these airports. These stories were surely apocryphal. Nonetheless, they circulated with frequency.

Although the workdays were long and confusing, the Lieutenant wasted no time in introducing me to the recreation available to servicemen at Palmerola. On the tenth, we went to one of the restaurants that the preventive medicine briefer had warned us about, the Pájaro Rojo in neighboring Comayagua. We ordered steaks ("If you have to eat out, get the meat well done; avoid pork and uncooked vegetables . . .").

The meal was the first of many similar ones that I would eat throughout the country. The little restaurant had at least one indoor dining room and several tables under an outside awning that gave way to a courtyard. A large brick-and-mortar brazier dominated the yard. The appetizer was *frijoles y tortillas*—refried beans and fresh corn-flour tortillas. The frijoles and tortillas were served in ceramic dishes atop another ceramic device that contained some glowing embers. A type of relish, composed of the dreaded uncooked vegetables, was served with the appetizer. The meat was a beefsteak that could easily have been made into combat boots. It came with French fries. The state of the meat made one eat even more of the frijoles and tortillas, which were constantly replenished. Hot sauce and catsup added to—or masked—the natural flavors. Large quantities of the local beers provided the social lubricant.

The next night, we sampled the fare at El Restaurante China, a true Chinese eatery run by immigrants in the mall, a small collection of shops on the ground floors of connected two-story buildings just off the main square of town. The village of Comayagua actually supported two authentic Chinese restaurants, but this one had the better reputation. Even so, the spring rolls tasted of rotten cabbage. Still, the quantities were huge. Eating there was a multicultural, multilingual experience. It was not uncommon to hear an order for *"Un* chicken chop suey, *por favor* ..."* There was also an element of danger in dining at El Restaurante China—it had a very small dining area, separated from the main thoroughfare of the mall only by a large glass window. It made a perfect terrorist target.

On the eleventh, the Sergeant First Class and I took the Technical Sergeant to Tegucigalpa to catch his plane out. On the twelfth, we took the Lieutenant to catch his flight, which was to leave early on the thirteenth. He planned on staying the night in the Maya Hotel, which, he explained, served as the principal accommodation for American transients. The Maya was a true luxury hotel with a small casino, bars, and two restaurants. The American forces kept a room reserved for servicemen caught in town overnight. Yet the standard procedure was to leave right before dusk in order to arrive right after darkness at PAB. It would have made more sense to stay in the luxurious Maya as the standing orders indicated. Evidently, upon their return to PAB, those who did stay were accused of freeloading. The prevailing sentiment seemed to be that if you followed the orders and stayed put in the capital, then you were "getting over" on all the others stuck in the hootches at Palmerola—based on the presumption that with a good plan, one should always be able to finish one's business and still have enough time to get back. The Technical Sergeant had neglected to tell me on that first night that we had had the opportunity to stay at the Maya.

The Maya room was also home to a young American who served as the task force duty driver. His mission was to transport personnel from PAB to the capital. This poor slob had to make two runs a day, and spent the rest of his time lounging at the hotel, all the while soaking up a massive amount of per diem, the daily expense money the military gives to servicemen. For staying free of charge in the Maya, this young soldier was picking up an extra $60 to $70 per day. Those of us assigned to the Spartan conditions of PAB received from $3.50 to $12.50, depending on our rank.

Upon hearing that JTFB had a duty driver, I was prompted to ask why the engineer vehicle had picked me up and why we had to take the Technical Sergeant and the Lieutenant to the airport ourselves. Why couldn't we use the duty driver? After much hemming and hawing about courtesy to incoming and outgoing personnel and having to waste too much time waiting on the duty vehicle, the Lieutenant got around to telling me that most of the sections that had their own vehicles also used such runs to pick up necessities from the embassy or the supermarkets, or to eat in a good, international restaurant. After spending some time in the bleak surroundings of PAB, I never again questioned the wisdom of these trips, despite the fact that, with so many Americans on the road in so many vehicles, good control was impossible. My mind kept wandering back to my pseudo-briefing on terrorism.

The Lieutenant had promised us a meal in the best restaurant in Honduras if we took him to the Maya. Unfortunately, we got lost on the way. In getting out of the mess, I learned my first important lesson about the Hondurans. We were tooling around in what passed for a middle-class neighborhood in Tegucigalpa—small, neat houses, constructed of block, with tile roofing—when we spotted a Honduran whittling outside his home. We asked directions in broken Spanish but couldn't understand his replies. All of a sudden, he had summoned his entire family of wife and several kids, loaded them into an old car, and motioned us to follow. He led us through the winding, congested streets to the hotel on the other side of the city. We tried to pay him for his trouble and his gas, but he adamantly refused. This was not the last time such courtesy would be extended to us.

The Lieutenant insisted that we eat at the Gaucho, a restaurant specializing in beef. I thought the meat I had wasn't so special, but I hadn't eaten anything except breakfast in Palmerola's mess hall yet, either. During the meal, an unusual thing happened. A young Honduran woman approached us and introduced herself as one of the Lieutenant's West Point classmates. She had been an exchange cadet who had spent all four years at the Academy and was now serving as a military police lieutenant at the Honduran Military Academy. Who would have thought that a supposedly backward, traditional country like Honduras would have sent one of the first women to West Point and then gainfully employed her upon return? She left us to our meat and our mutterings about small and strange worlds.

After the meal, we dropped the Lieutenant off and headed back to Palmerola. It was dark already, and for the second time in less than a week, I was breaking security regulations. Only by sheer luck, did we find our way out of the city and back on the road to Palmerola. The Sergeant First Class and I were drained by the hectic five days that served to get us to, and immerse us in, the life at JTFB. It had been a bewildering period of learning and adapting.

11 January 1986, PAB

The place smells not at all unusual, except near the trashcans or latrines. This poor country is definitely approaching the saturation point of population. So many live in mud or scrap-wood shacks between the roads and private fence lines. Before long, they'll start moving to the cities in desperation. Right now, the poor appear to be still fairly self-sufficient, but only God knows how. Some of the easily reached areas of the hillsides have been deforested. However, the second growth is thick. Pines grow faster here than in the United States.

Honduras has few wealthy people and a small middle class; most people live similar existences. Not for long, though, due to the population explosion which threatens to create a mass of the "most poor." When that happens, even the smallest landowner will be looked at covetously. For sure, all the contracting we do here helps the local employers and workers. We spend hundreds of thousands here on construction and utilities.

Radical theorists maintain that the underdeveloped nature of the lesser developed countries (LDCs) is a direct result of the capitalist world economy. This group of theories even has a catchy name—Dependency Theory. Supposedly, the LDCs were first held in colonial bondage. As the European countries disengaged from the colonies or were thrown out, the newly independent nations were still held in economic bondage. They were

36

forced to be the markets for goods produced in the metropolitan centers. As the theory goes, when entrepreneurs sought to build factories in LDCs, they were nonetheless condemned by the theorists and like-minded intellectuals for exploiting cheap labor and local resources to satiate the markets in Europe and America.

The most recent phase of radical condemnation focused on loan debt and technology control. The radicals maintain that it was imperialistic for banks to "force" loans on unsuspecting Third World countries, and equally imperialistic to ask those countries to pay back the loans. As technology is important for any country to advance into the modern age, it is also imperialistic that only a handful of nations serve as the font of technological development, forcing poorer countries to pay for life- enhancing machines.

Hence, it did not matter to radicals whether cheap goods were made in the capitalistic North and sold to the South, or vice versa. Nor did it matter whether loans and technology were easy or hard to come by. What bothered the radicals of any continent was capitalism and the fruits it brought to those countries that wholeheartedly embraced it. Cuba was supposed to provide an alternative example of development, especially for Latin Americans who had for so long been lackeys of the Spanish, the British, and the Americans. This was the forceful example behind the communist movements in Central America in the 1980s—despite the fact that Cuba was far more dependent on the Soviet Union than it ever had been on the United States during the heyday of gambling, prostitution, and rum-running, and despite the fact that Cubans were sent abroad in the tens of thousands to fight the proxy wars of the USSR.

According to Dependency Theory, not all of the poverty that I had seen by the eleventh of January was the result of overpopulation, inadequate infrastructure, or ignorance. It was the direct result of American capitalist control over the Honduran economy, an economy run for the benefit of overweight American housewives who wanted cheap bananas. Radical theory proclaimed that the only way to overcome the poverty was through an overthrow of the capitalist system, which required revolution. For the sane among us, a few schoolhouses and roads would have done wonders immediately, at far less human cost.

14 January 1986, PAB
My second day on the job as the only officer present in engineering.

Last night I worked until 0030 hours. Designed my first structure—a stage for the upcoming USO show, one of those "can't-wait, must-do, hot" projects. Found it hard to visualize the stage in my drawings. Never did get them to scale, but did better than I ever expected.

16 January 1968, PAB

SFC(P)—the P is for promotable from E7 to E8. Male Caucasian. Combat vet. Experienced. Humorous. Claims to have been married four times, once to a black girl in New York City. Born in Newburgh, New York. Grew up in North Carolina, but lived his last few years as a civilian in Newburgh working at West Point as barracks police (BP)—a janitor—and as the commandant's driver. Says he was first married at age sixteen. Claims nine kids as his own, even though never married for more than a few months at a time.

The first few days he had good ideas and seemed to want to work hard. Now he only takes care of issuing and reordering materials for self-help, though I could use him for planning. I doubt if ordering him to do designs or contracts would do much good. We'll see.

I'm getting to know my hootch mates better. Most are average inoffensive types. One, though, is an arrogant little infantry martinet, mad at the world but sure of his own superiority.

As usual, I live on the edge as I try to make a name for myself in my new position. I can tell that all the other staff officers are scoping me out for threats, pliability to their views, sociability (drinking, dancing, swearing, womanizing), and last of all, competence and professionalism. Every little slip expands out of proportion in my mind, but I sense progress through the back door.

My work is so time-consuming and mentally draining that all I'm noticing are my immediate surroundings.

My first hootch mates were a varied lot. We all brought with us the pride and prejudices of our arms (Army and Air Force), branches (USAF weather service, Army Aviation, Finance Corps, Engineers, Infantry), and personal backgrounds.

The infantry officer was a Captain, class of '76 from USMA, and worried about making major. Since he was approaching ten years of service and had not yet been selected, he thought his prospects looked dim. His father had been the former commander of the U.S. MILGROUP in Tegucigalpa where he had attended high school. He was serving as the assistant J3 (task force operations officer).

The Infantry Captain functioned as the task force asshole. Some people are made into assholes by the positions they occupy in the military. This guy was a natural one. It wouldn't have mattered whether he was an Army Officer or an investment banker, he would have been an A-number-one asshole. He couldn't stand most people, especially if they were not in the infantry or if they were mere lieutenants. His constant comments about his roommates were "dickhead lieutenants," "dumbass engineers," "fuckin' Air Force wienies," or other such constructions. He was even harder on those who didn't share our hootch. No one measured up to his standards except for the one or two people he selected to commiserate with. Not surprisingly, his main companion was a bitter, burned-out officer, who as a major had been passed over twice for promotion and faced retirement, something that rarely happened to Army Officers of that time. The two of them were a joy to be around. To his credit, the Infantry Captain recognized his position in the world. As he put it, "I'm the task force asshole. Every organization needs one, and I'm the one here."

Another hootchmate, the staff weather officer (SWO for short), was in the Air Force, and couldn't abide the primitive living conditions, even though he had one of the only air-conditioned offices on Palmerola (his instruments had to be kept cool). He also refused to see any purpose in our being in Central America at all. He was one-half Huron Indian, and one-half second generation Hungarian.

The hootch also had another Captain from the 9th Infantry Division. He was a very soft-spoken and amiable pilot of U-H1H HUEY utility helicopters. He became the JTFB Headquarters and Headquarters Company (HHC) commander.

The junior man in Hootch A35 was a Second Lieutenant who had grown up a poor Cajun. He served a hitch in the Army as an enlisted man before going to college. He was an Airborne-qualified Finance officer who handled the accounts for JTFB. He had something of the feeling of inferiority common to most new officers but was in excellent physical condition and was superb in his work. He also had an inquiring mind and read as much history as he could get his hands on.

Then, there was the First Lieutenant and fellow Engineer that worked in my office. His father was a retired career officer. His mother was a Nisei. He had grandparents who still lived on a small farm in Japan. He graduated from a Joplin, Missouri, high school, went on to graduate near the top of his West Point class in '84, and did fine engineering work. He was stable and quite unflappable.

Life in the hootch centered on the clash of personalities. The Infantry Captain continually hazed the lieutenants, and raged about most things in general, but especially lieutenants, and increasingly, Engineers. The SWO complained just about being there. The Huey pilot mostly kept quiet but told interesting stories about the horses he raised on his miniature farm outside of Fort Lewis. The lieutenants suffered, but not silently. I just tried to fit in, succeeding and failing alternatingly. Even so, a camaraderie developed rather quickly, born of common sacrifice and living in close proximity.

One of the first lessons I learned in Palmerola engineering was the serious nature of power outages. Palmerola received its electrical power straight from the Honduran power grid running through our area, but the power went out with maddening regularity. When it did, PAB's water pumps and chlorination station stopped working. Consequently, water was in short supply. The showers and the twenty flush toilets were immediately closed, and morale would immediately plummet. The few small generators on base supplied only enough power to run important signal and security equipment. Sometimes the power would be off for as long as forty-eight hours. Even after restoration, water would stay rationed until a sufficient reserve was built up in the system's single twenty-two-thousand-gallon tank.

When the power went out, we Engineers became the least favorite people on base. Even the technically minded failed to understand why the soldiers and airmen in our office couldn't just run out and fix the power. "Goddamn stupid-ass engineers," was a common muttering. Unfortunately, the Engineer office had neither the appropriate technicians nor the authority to affect power outages.

We did develop, though, an answer for the constant questioning, at least at night. If the nearby village was also dark at night, then we could confidently reply that the power outage was widespread and would get fixed as soon as the Honduran power company found the problem. If the village was still lighted, then the problem was internal to the base, and the civilian base-maintenance contractor would find and fix the problem. Until nightfall, though, we had to make do with "I don't know."

Palmerola's base camp had been wired for power distribution mainly through contracts with local Honduran firms. Shortly after completion of the projects, the task force discovered that the work had been marginal at best. Transformers blew regularly around the camp. The Honduran companies had done no better for themselves, because outages in the surrounding area were also quite frequent.

Why rely on the Hondurans to wire an American camp? Aside from the political and economic reasons, the main reason was that the Army had few power distribution specialists (highline wiremen) on active duty. Most of the active duty soldiers were inexperienced privates and Spec Fours. Each combat heavy battalion had a few, but there was generally little work for them to do in garrison. Consequently, most of the soldiers in this field (military occupational specialty (MOS) 52G at the time) left active duty for more lucrative civilian work in the same field. Only when we needed them in a place like Honduras did the Army discover how vulnerable it was. Power distribution would remain one of the Engineer office's major challenges throughout my stay.

5
SETTLING IN

For to win one hundred victories in one hundred battles is not the acme of skill. To subdue the enemy without fighting is the acme of skill.

—SUN TZU

If the political aims are small, the motives slight and tensions low, a prudent general may look for any way to avoid major crises and decisive actions, exploit any weaknesses in the opponent's military and political strategy, and finally reach a peaceful settlement . . . But he must never forget that he is moving along devious paths where the god of war may catch him unawares.

—CLAUSEWITZ

20 January, Martin Luther King Day, PAB
Kind of quiet the last two days. Getting to know my hootch mates better. Still haven't changed my original impressions. I can tell I'm already becoming too closeted here. I need to get out of PAB-Comayagua to some of the historical sites. I need to read some of the local papers if possible. At Comayagua two nights ago, I heard two GIs cussing at the begging children. The children knew gutter English very well. They even knew the N word, which they used correctly and often when they failed to obtain any coins (it's wisely prohibited to give anything to the begging kids). This angered one black sergeant who was mostly upset that someone (some racist white) had taught the kids that word. Yet, ironically, he had been cussing the kids and calling them all kinds of names before they used the N word, thus contributing in large measure to that which he heartily disliked. We must do all that we can to avoid such things, but I suppose it is inevitable when people are away from home so long that they forget they are guests and start treating the natives as they would a

neighborhood pest back home. Still, most of the troops seem very sensitive at this point. I've seen very few anti-Honduran attitudes so far. Post-Vietnam effect I guess.

By the time I had been at PAB for two weeks, the normal procedures became clearer as did the average behavior of our troops and officers. The Army has a saying that "We train as we'll fight." Rarely do you hear the obvious corollary "That we'll fight as we train." The military effort in Honduras in the 1980s was conducted in a low-intensity-conflict (LIC) environment. LIC was the latest variant in the mid-1980s of what was once called small wars, partisan operations, guerrilla war, or counterinsurgency—depending on the era and the conflict. Upon my deployment to Honduras, I began hearing this strange phrase for the first time. I had had no training in such a conflict, nor, from what I could tell, had most of the others at PAB.

America has waged many "operations short of war," "small wars," or "low-intensity conflicts." We cut our teeth fighting this way against American Indians. Our first taste of Asian LIC was in the Philippine Insurrection that ensued after their liberation in the Spanish-American War. The numerous interventions in the Caribbean also should have increased our database. In the 1940s and 1950s, we aided the Greeks and the Turks, and then the Filipinos again. The 1960s saw the LIC efforts reach their zenith with President Kennedy's emphasis on special operations forces and counterinsurgency doctrine.

The world continued to change, though. Most of our involvement in such matters had been directed against insurgencies. In the 1980s, we also had to focus on pro-insurgency operations in Angola, Afghanistan, and Nicaragua in addition to preventing insurgencies in places like Honduras.

Low-intensity conflict was a phrase often used and rarely defined in U.S. doctrine. It was not as easy to say what LIC meant as it was to describe where it usually occurred (in the Third World as the Lesser Developed Countries were also known) or against whom it was usually fought (some force using insurgent tactics). But, throughout the 1980s, the Army had a manual for LIC, Field Manual (FM) 100-20, *Low Intensity Conflict,* published in 1981. Unfortunately for the operations in

Honduras through 1986, this manual was not standard fare in the officer and NCO training courses. The bulk of U.S. operational focus was centered in Europe opposite the heavily armored Warsaw Pact forces. We also had a division with supporting air forces deployed in the defense of South Korea, but it, too, was trained for modern force-on-force warfare. Therefore, throughout the Army, the focus of the training was on these missions. The inevitable result was the deployment of soldiers and airmen to Central America who were not prepared adequately to function in the environment they found.

"Doctrine is the *accepted* body of ideas concerning war, especially the organization and training for the conduct of war."[20] The Army issued two editions of its basic operations manual in the eighties. Both were tremendous improvements over their predecessors. Each claimed to address the fundamental issues of fighting, regardless of the nature of the conflict. Yet it was necessary to augment such a general manual with other manuals covering specific operations. This was the case with Field Manual (FM) 100-20, *Low Intensity Conflict*. Also, whatever the pretext, the "why" for an operation or a conflict, the doctrine represents the "how."

According to FM 100-20, our operations in Honduras took place in an LIC environment, type B. That is, "Internal defense and development assistance operations involving U.S. advice, combat support, and combat service support for indigenous or allied forces engaged in establishing, regaining, or maintaining control of specific land areas threatened by guerrilla warfare, revolution, subversion, or other tactics aimed at internal seizure of power." The goal was "building viable institutions—political, military, economic, and social . . ."[21] Not only was Honduras threatened by the Sandinista buildup, but it could also be considered to be in the "latent and incipient phase" of its own insurgency.[22] Organized groups, as shown in the historical section above, had committed acts of political violence and had declared themselves dedicated to the overthrow of the government.

The U.S. doctrine, as produced in the FM, focused on combating insurgency, which was by far the knottiest problem in LIC. Yet, several key parts of the book centered on preventing insurgency, or ensuring that it did not go beyond the incipient phase. These methods included

44

economic, political, and military components, but their intended effect was psychological. Such a program sought to promote a favorable attitude in friendly, hostile, or neutral groups towards the U.S. forces and the host government, thus dampening the potential for violent rebellion.[23]

Even though many of our Honduran operations supported the building of a military infrastructure for internal or external defense, all operations should have been undertaken with the view of establishing and maintaining the proper attitudes among American servicemen toward the population and ensuring appropriate relations between our troops and the population. The hackneyed and much maligned phrase "winning the hearts and minds of the people" was still appropriate. Our actions were an attempt at what could have been called "preventive nation-building."

Another helpful doctrinal component found in the FM was the military civic-action project—designed to meet some local need such as a well or road, but one where the local populace had to take part. It would do no good to create a welfare mentality by having American labor, materials, and expertise do all the work. Any such project, like so many well-intentioned ones implemented in the Third World by development agencies over the last few decades, would eventually fall into disrepair because upkeep would exceed the capabilities of the citizens, or it would become stigmatized as an example of Yankee imperialism. Rather, a properly designed and executed project augmented local skills, used locally available materials, and further, sought to promote local or national pride through the effort. In these ways, the manner of execution of our tasks and the manner of treatment of the host population by our troops became as important as any purely military show of force.

Although it wasn't apparent at the time, and certainly wasn't explained very well to those serving in Honduras, certain wise policies were already in place and having a good effect. All GIs had to convert their money to Honduran *lempira* upon arriving at PAB. All transactions on the base were conducted in *lempira* ("limps" was the slang term) in order not to subvert the local money supply with dollars. The prohibition against giving to beggars meant that parents would not resent us for degrading their kids.

On the other hand, as the policies on liberty and prostitutes and the name-calling incident indicated, we were not yet where we should have been. Our orders may have said that we were just augmenting U.S. forces in Honduras or that we were traveling for training purposes, but we were really involved in a low-intensity environment. Since we had not been specifically trained for the mission, perhaps it is no wonder we did not do it as effectively as we should have.

Although the LIC manual existed, I had never seen it. The training scenarios used at West Point and in my Officer Basic Course (OBC) were oriented toward armored and mechanized units fighting similarly armed foes from the Warsaw Pact. That we might have to be involved in operations short of war, especially in a low-intensity-conflict environment, was not emphasized at all, despite the recent example of the Grenada contingency operation. I suspect that this was true of most of the officer and NCO courses of the early and mid-1980s. In like manner, the first American troops sent to Korea in 1950 had been used for occupation duties in Japan. And most of the troops sent to Vietnam in the early years came from units that had been training to fight the Soviets in Central Europe. Hence, one could say that we were following a well-worn path of American arms—we had not been trained for the conflict confronting us.

After a while, I came to realize that we weren't as sensitive as I first presumed on Martin Luther King's birthday. The lack of sensitivity did stem from the amount of time spent on the ground. The longer one was at Palmerola, the more one used the word *"Hondo."* At first, Hondo was a useful shortening of Honduran. With time, the word became a pejorative. In *The Grapes of Wrath,* a character talks about the word *"Okie"* in the same way. It's not the word; it's how people say it that counts. Towards the end of my six months in Honduras, I heard Hondo used in some pretty unfriendly ways. What caused American anger or resentment at the Hondurans? The primitiveness of the facilities; the separation from friends, family, and normal routine—the Hondurans became convenient scapegoats for these facts of life.

For example, Palmerola had a little post exchange (PX). The Honduran officers had privileges there (why they used it I don't know, considering their wages and our prices). Honduran employees also ran the place. Whenever the PX got in a few highly desirable items, which it occasionally did, the Honduran officers always seemed to be in the PX before the bulk of Americans. The common assumption was that the PX workers tipped them off, and the Hondurans would get first crack at the goods. The Honduran PX workers could be seen drinking and eating some of the goods while at their cash registers or while waiting to stock shelves. The assumption here was that they hadn't paid for the items. Agreed that these are not great crimes in comparison to what goes on in the world, but to the legalistic minds of most Americans, these acts smacked of corruption and unfairness when in fact the extension of PX privileges to Honduran officers was a simple and cheap goodwill gesture, and the local PX workers almost certainly were paying for their items. Couple these bad assumptions, though, with incidents involving beggars or minor thievery, and too many of us became ready to condemn the entire country.

If anything, the concepts of our LIC doctrine would argue that American troops need to walk on eggshells over such matters. Why should our soldiers, serving in a hostile, austere environment, accept such minor insults from foreign nationals—especially when we're serving to protect them? Well, first I would say that "accept" is the wrong word. We don't have to accept them. What we do have to do is learn to live with them. What we see as corruption or unfairness may be culturally acceptable to others. In such situations, Americans walk a fine line between imposing our values on others and providing the support necessary to allow native institutions to develop in desirable ways. An overly negative reaction is sure to provoke resentment and play into the hands of our enemies.

In 1914, Mexican officials arrested some unarmed American sailors in the port of Vera Cruz. The commander of the U.S. naval squadron considered this and other similar actions unacceptable. He shelled the city. President Wilson, a politician who often professed his love for peace and for teaching others the benefits of democracy, supported the commander and then authorized the landing of several thousand U.S. troops. Over one hundred Mexicans died, and American forces occupied Vera Cruz for nine months. You don't have to be a genius to gauge the effect this had on Latin American acceptance of Wilsonian values.

Again, the problem for those of us at PAB was that few of us had been trained in the very real subtleties required by our doctrine.

22 *January*, *PAB*

Lieutenant Colonel H and Captain D came in yesterday. Lieutenant Colonel H has been a big help in beating down the meanies and in giving suggestions. He came from the DCS (deputy chief of staff) engineer office in the Army command in Panama. Captain D has built and operated several tent cities. Before that, he was in USAF base civil engineering. His is the voice of authority. His experience allows him to do and say things I cannot say or do. No matter how much someone respects effort, they will respect expertise more. Hopefully, I can gain some practical civil engineering experience here.

PAB, Honduras is an anomaly—unique in that it is the first operational base camp that I'm aware of us building since Vietnam. Everyone realizes that we're guests. Yet we maintain the attitude that we have a right and a responsibility to be here and stay here. Unfortunately, most see only PAB and their jobs and do not understand the wider significance of our actions here.

Lieutenant Colonel Rivera, our Honduran liaison at the Honduran Air Force Academy on Palmerola, must approve whatever we build or what land we use. The air is filled with tension whenever this subject comes up—how do we get him to agree to what we want, even if it is as typically American, and as typically unnecessary, as a swimming pool (once suggested for approval purposes as a "fire reservoir")?

Previous staffers at the engineer office had successfully upgraded and fenced a baseball/softball field. Another successful mission had been the upgrading, fencing, and lighting of a tennis court and the installation of basketball goals at either end. Other such issues we worked on from time to time included racquetball courts ("Won't we need air conditioning? Might have to build the one-walled Latin American version." "Yeah, but Americans won't play." "Well, at least it would keep the Hondurans happy, and wouldn't cost nearly as much"), and a joint officers club on the bank of the Honduran commander's fishpond. Work on these projects ate up precious time. Luckily, during my stay, Congress never agreed to waste funds on such projects. I found them impossible to justify when we could have spent the money on drilling wells or building schools and clinics in our nation-building operations.

One of the first missions I observed the Lieutenant work on was the installation of a small concrete pad as a foundation of the Armed Forces Radio and Television System (AFRTS) satellite dish. Lieutenant Colonel Rivera considered this permanent construction. Because most of the American structures on Palmerola were constructed out of unseasoned lumber, they would assuredly be gone through rot in a few tropical seasons. Concrete pads, however, were forever. America's record for continuing military support for non-Europeans being less than stellar, the Hondurans did not want a bunch of ruins littering their landscape when our training mission ended. Approval of the AFRTS pad required our USAF lieutenant colonel to talk to Rivera personally.

The same Honduran attitude seriously affected the construction of bunkers. The Hondurans would not let us dig in. All our bunkers had to be above ground, which immediately reduced aspects of concealment and frontal cover. Many bunkers of varying quality had already been built when I arrived. The Lieutenant and I set out to standardize construction and maximize protection. We dug out a design from a publication of the Army Engineer School. The design had been used on firebases in Vietnam. The bunkers consisted of parallel rows of fifty-five-gallon drums filled with dirt or sand to serve as walls and supports. A six-foot-radius, corrugated-metal-pipe (CMP) culvert-half was then placed on top of the rows of barrels to serve as a roof. Finally, the structure was covered on all sides and on top with at least three feet of sandbags. A sandbag blast wall covered both ends of the bunker but allowed easy entrance and exit. I made the Lieutenant officer-in-charge (OIC) of bunkers. He eventually oversaw the construction or reconstruction of fifty-five such bunkers during his tenure.

Standardizing the bunkers proved to be the easy part. The military of the mid-1980s disdained hard manual labor. Palmerola had no troops available just to perform labor details. Most of the soldiers and airmen specialized in some field such as logistics, medical services, or aviation. Detachment and section commanders continually grumbled about having to build or rebuild bunkers (the sandbags rotted after a few months)—that is, when they didn't just refuse. Bunker building was the work of the Infantry or, better yet, the Engineers, they would exclaim. Yet, our tiny Engineer office couldn't come close to providing the manpower necessary.

The worst complainers were always the USAF personnel. "Hey, we're not building any bunkers! We're in the Air Force," I heard time and again when the Lieutenant would make one of his periodic state-of-the-bunkers reports.

"Someone has to build the bunker," I'd reply. "It's in your area, and your people will use it in case of attack."

"Nobody is likely to attack us here, and you know it. Besides, the Army's supposed to build the bunkers for the Air Force so that we can carry on doing what we're trained to do."

"I suspect the Marines in Beirut didn't expect an attack either three years ago. Again, the bunker is yours, and your people are going to build it."

"Well, can't you contract to have it done?"

"There's nowhere near enough money!"

Normally, the USAF contingent commander, the AFFOR, or his Army counterpart, the ARFOR, would have to give a direct order to the section involved to get them to respond. The Engineer office bought hundreds of barrels and tons of sand for the construction effort. It was not unusual to see a group of forty or fifty people sweating under the tropical sun in a human chain passing sandbags to a few stackers. If the stackers were good, they produced nice, neat, and tightly packed rows. If the workers were lackadaisical or careless, perhaps because they resented the labor involved, the final product had bulges, half-filled bags, and was loosely packed. Consequently, with a few rains the bunker walls almost always fell, necessitating reconstruction. Life at Palmerola had its little justices.

26 January 1986 PAB Superbowl Sunday
Raining hard now. There is a bite to the air.

George Bush arrived today for the swearing in of the new, fairly elected civilian president Jose Azcona. I shook the vice president's hand. I'd probably vote for him if he ran. He told a joke about the recent Geneva Summit: "A Russian and an American were arguing over who had the most freedom. The American said that he was so free that he could stand in front of the White House and yell, 'To hell with Ronald Reagan!' The Russian replied, 'That's nothing special. I can stand in front of the Kremlin and yell "To hell with Ronald Reagan," too.' "

50

Glad the Bears won. I thoroughly enjoyed their guts and willingness to take risks on what we would have called "fun" plays— running a QB option, or running a 308-pound fullback/defensive tackle.

Oddity of the day: our intelligence briefings seem to be taken from the front page of the previous day's Miami Herald.

The vice president's visit caused a flurry of activity in our office. The task force command group decided that we needed a podium, a raised platform, and a set of portable steps for the entourage. We were ordered to come up with these items in only a couple of days.

A half-dozen combat engineers had arrived at Palmerola as the advance party for a DFT (deployment for training) from Fort Devens, Massachusetts. We put them to work building steps out of available lumber, to be used for those dignitaries descending from helicopters. They built ugly but functional steps out of four-by-fours in the engineer yard.

The podium and platform exceeded our capabilities. Additionally, we did not have the time to send out the requisite bid requests to three different contractors as required by U.S. contract law and Army regulations. Luckily, the base maintenance firm's contract allowed it to accept sole-source bids for jobs estimated at less than a thousand dollars. Our office estimated that the job would be in the two-hundred-to-three-hundred-dollar range. The contractor submitted a bid for $999, and we had no choice but to accept due to the impending arrival. This was to be a common occurrence when similar situations arose in the future.

Ironically, after the podium and platform were built, the command group decided that the podium was too unbecoming and scrounged a portable podium set with built-in microphone and speakers. At least the platform was used. The Devens contingent was also quite gratified that no less a personage than Barbara Bush used its steps, which wobbled noticeably only once.

A number of troops had been allowed on the flight line to see the Vice President and the congressmen in the delegation. Mr. Bush spent more than an hour passing affably through the crowd, shaking hands and posing for pictures. One young Democrat congressman from Oklahoma was almost eager in his efforts to meet as many of the servicemen as possible.

During the handshaking, a loudmouthed National Guard private was showing a card to his buddies and bragging about how he was going to present it to the Vice President. I got a look at the card simultaneously with a Bush staffer. The card had some offensive statement about calling the guardsman's unit if death, destruction, pillaging, and burning were required. The staffer promptly "asked" the private that he didn't really want to give such trash to the vice president of the United States, did he? Once the attention of several NCOs, officers, and vice-presidential handlers turned on him, the private guessed not.

The task force headquarters personnel watched the Super Bowl on a large-screen TV hooked up to the Headquarters and Headquarters Company (HHC) satellite dish. The TV was mounted under a huge covered patio (called a *bohio* in Honduran Spanish) that served as the headquarters common area. One of those odd dry-season cold fronts had moved in, reducing the temperature from the nineties into the low sixties. Watching the game was actually kind of miserable in that weather. At least the game was live. AFRTS did not carry the game until a couple of weeks later.

28 January 1986 PAB

Finding my way into my job. Still far too much to do. The main problem with Engineer deployments for training (DFT) is that either JTFB, SOUTHCOM, or the 193d has requested too many of them for the middle quarters of this year—eight more than are actually going to happen. There also exists the problem of verbal promises to the Hondurans. They take them as the word of honor among gentlemen.

The Hondurans passed power from one civilian to another yesterday—the first time in over fifty years. Ironically, the Reagan administration will not get any accolades for it, or for Guatemala, El Salvador, Uruguay, or Argentina. They will get blamed for any abuses of democracy in Chile, or the Philippines, or South Africa.

A day at PAB began at 0530 hours for most folks. On Monday, Wednesday, and Friday, the Army troops formed up for physical training (PT) at this time. If you were intelligent, you slept in your PT gear so that all you had to do was put on socks and shoes. This meant that you could stay in the sack until 0520 at least. When I first arrived, the USAF personnel were supposed to join us in PT. This requirement generated a great deal of friction between the two services. Evidently, the USAF physical standards were lower than those of the Army, so many of the USAF officers and NCOs ignored the requirement. Hence, the USAF personnel rarely did PT, but they found it impossible to sleep with the Army coming and going. Most got up and headed to the showers to beat the rush. Eventually Air Force participation was formally dropped as a requirement. The only people who complained about it were those Army personnel in such bad shape that they welcomed having the airmen to look down upon.

The Army went through desultory calisthenics on the gravel parking lot, grass being a valued commodity. The gravel did make push-ups and sit-ups painful, though. Then, the Army formed up for a two- or three-mile run. The group was small, but there was always someone who thought cadence had to be sung. He usually sang alone, as the rest of us concentrated on breathing and surviving. After the run, many headed to a makeshift exercise area where our earlier counterparts had constructed chin-up bars and a sit-up bench.

After PT came a hurried "navy shower," so named because our water was rationed, just as it was on most ships. One wet down quickly, and then turned the water off to soap up. The water was turned back on for a quick rinse. Not using too much soap was the key.

Next was breakfast, if one chose, at one of the two PAB mess halls ran by an American company called Harbert. These hootch facilities were always hot and muggy, even though huge fans were available. Often the Honduran servers, dressed in their incongruous cook's whites and hats, would be sweating into the food. Still, a good meal of omelets, bacon, pancakes, and home fries could generally be had. The only thing missing was fresh milk. The substitute was ultra-heat-treated milk with an unrefrigerated shelf life of three months. If the ice machines were on the blink, the UHT milk was lukewarm. Lunch and dinner meals were largely forgettable, except for the salad bars of safe, fresh vegetables. On Sunday, lunch was hamburgers or cheeseburgers, and the lines were always long for this American delicacy.

For some reason the Harbert mess hall on the western side of the air base, known as Camp Blackjack, had a better reputation than the other one. Both were run by Harbert. Both were managed by retired Army mess sergeants, doing the same job they had been doing for decades, but getting paid better as civilians. Both got their food from the same sources, and both had Hondurans as cooks and servers. Yet, the psychology of the serviceman is not always logical. Someone probably once declared that the aviators and logistics troops on Blackjack had better food, perhaps because they were involved in supply and transport and, therefore, could take first pick on the rations. This assertion, or one like it, became accepted as fact. The crowds got so large on Blackjack, and the traffic so heavy on the perimeter road that the command had to issue an edict requiring troops to eat only on their own side of base.

The morning staff meeting was at 0730, Mondays through Fridays. Although Saturday was a workday, no meeting was usually held. All commanders and section leaders attended. It was a procession of reports on the whole of Central America with a special focus on Honduras, personnel and logistical statistics, and operational updates from all the forces in country. The meeting then broke up, and the various chiefs returned to their sections to accomplish whatever piece of the operation belonged to them.

The formal workday ended about 1700 hours. The Engineer office normally stayed open later, as did operations. The communications sections maintained around-the-clock staffing. Although one might find a small barbecue or drinking session on one of the patios or decks many occupants had added to their hootches, the evenings were mostly occupied by TV.

On military bases the world over at the time, the Armed Force Radio and Television Service (AFRTS) offered a meager fare. PAB boasted at least three satellite dishes, though, and until the signals were scrambled about halfway through my tour, the troops picked up all the movie channels. Regular TV or AFRTS programming was horrid in comparison.

This situation was greatly remedied by one engineering NCO who set up his own network. He strung about thirty of the hootches together with coaxial cable scrounged from the signal unit. He created a network connected to a VCR he'd acquired. He had his girlfriend send down a box of movie tapes, and he set up a schedule of viewing. Every night at 2130, he would put on a skin flick. At that time, almost everyone was glued to the screens, debating how well Debbie was doing Dallas, or the relative merits of one porn queen versus another.

Sunday was the official day of rest, in that the sections only worked if they had to, which they often did, especially during the military exercise season. PAB had a contingent of chaplains that operated out of a chapel- hootch. Yet, strangely for an isolated post, very few attended services. The head chaplain was a Catholic reservist who kept extending his tour. He probably knew more about Palmerola Air Base than anybody in uniform. His assistants were of various denominations, all Protestant. I attended a couple of services and found them lackluster. No more than a dozen worshipers showed up. One of the NCOs from another part of base brought along his guitar and sang some contemporary gospel, or rock-gospel, songs. Somehow the service had all the flavor of a radio show presided over by the chief DJ, Father John Pepsi Cola.

Perhaps I am too harsh on the chaplains. They had to compete for attention with all of the secular attractions of PAB and the surrounding countryside. On the other hand, maybe this says volumes about the decline in the spiritual nature of young Americans in the mid-1980s. I do know that I rarely saw the chaplains except for the Sunday services I attended and one other time when a young Nazarene chaplain came to ask for a donation of scrap lumber to help build a house for a Honduran peasant. When he'd been an enlisted man, the chaplain had held MOS 12B, combat engineer, so maybe he didn't mind coming to our office to ask for help. I had expected the chaplains to be decisively engaged in activities that built bridges between the troops and the surrounding communities. Perhaps they were, but it was not obvious to this casual observer.

Most people just slept late on Sunday. My hootch-mates and I and a few others generally played basketball on the Honduran Academy's tennis court, fighting our way through the smoke of the burning latrine wastes when the winds shifted. Sunday afternoon was prime time for beer busts, and that was the only time I ever saw ethnic animosity openly expressed.

Blacks, whites, and Hispanics were the largest groups represented in the U.S. forces at PAB. On Sundays, after living and working together for six days, the three main groups would split up. One could easily find one group or another sacrificing a yard bird to the god of smoke - barbecuing chicken—and drinking beer. Soon the music competition began, with contemporary rock trying to blast its way through more soulful music or music with a Latin beat. Cries of "Turn that shit off, man!" "Get rid of the jungle music!" or *"Chinga tu madre!"* would break out. If the Celtics were playing on Sunday—especially if they were playing the Detroit Pistons or Houston Rockets—this was also a time of black and white insensitivity, barely muted below the level of a direct challenge or insult. I remember no openly racial incidents, but cross-cultural tensions there were.

29 January 1986 PAB

The day after the shuttle Challenger blew up, I watched it over and over again. I felt sick at first—so many lives, so much national pride and energy, gone so quickly. I really felt my own mortality. Clausewitz, I think, said the moral is to the physical as three is to one, and that the killing of courage is far more important than the killing of men. Well, sights like Challenger's destruction make serious dents in my moral armor. To die so quickly, without performing any glorious deeds on the direct path to death, seems such a disheartening waste.

Went to the TACAN [a navigational device for in-coming aircraft] site up on the nearest ridge, sixty-six hundred feet up. Pretty sparse and cold and rainy. "Just like a Vietnam fire base," I heard it described. Cliffs on two sides. A couple of overland routes of attack possible. A platoon of MPs had the guard. Their bunkers were bad—not interlocking, roofs too thin, wire too close. My job was to scout the pig trail [road] for upgrade. It definitely needs it, but how the equipment will get there and how the necessary fill material will get there mystifies me. I'll take the company commander from B Co, 39th Engr. Bn. to the site. He's a licensed professional engineer (PE). Maybe he can figure it out.

The road to the TACAN site rose out of a little village, La Paz, which was the home of Honduras's outgoing president, Roberto Suazo Córdova. La Paz was across the valley from PAB, about the same distance as Comayagua. Suazo Córdova had placed it off-limits for U.S.

recreational purposes. The road to the TACAN site corkscrewed upward from La Paz for ten miles at a slope approaching 7 percent in some places. It was a dirt track barely wide enough for one vehicle, and had at least two ninety-degree turns. In places, washouts narrowed the road even further. At the ten-mile point lay the beginning of the trail to the site. The trail twisted for another two miles at a gentler slope, but was in such a poor state that it made the main road seem a highway. The trail was a point of contention for it also led to the house of the man who rented us the land for the TACAN site. He wanted it upgraded.

The garrison and technicians on the TACAN site subsisted mainly on the fuel, water, and food flown up to them by helicopter. The winds on top of this ridge were vicious and unpredictable. When weather socked in the site, no supplies came, and the troops were miserable. If the trail could be upgraded to the point where many of the supplies could be trucked up, the cost savings would be remarkable. A CH-47 Chinook helicopter cost an estimated thirty-five hundred dollars per hour to operate, a UH-60 Blackhawk somewhat less. With an improved road, trucks could accomplish the resupply mission for a very small fraction of the cost.

Unfortunately, the trail needed major repairs. At least eleven culverts were needed to control drainage. Areas of the trail that were already washed out required either retaining walls or further side hill cuts to create a new roadbed. All of these required heavy pieces of equipment, but the equipment would have to "walk" up the ten miles to the trail's beginning. That would be a truly slow and tortuous climb for a bulldozer, backhoe, or earthmover. There was no way to haul the equipment up such slopes and around hairpin curves on lowboy trailers.

I tried to arrange for some work to be done on the trail with each "deployment for training" (DFT) that came to Palmerola. Generally, the commanders were not happy to be asked to climb their equipment to the site. One battalion commander stated flatly that he did not want his unit involved. "What would I do if the dozers broke down halfway up?" he asked plaintively. My unspoken, mental reply was "Dammit, fix them on the spot, sir!" Peacetime caution had stunted his thinking. To the credit of the 39th and 27th Engineers, two units that spent several weeks at PAB in 1986, they gave me as much aid as they could spare.

On my first trip to the TACAN site, and on every subsequent one, I saw the effect of misplaced compassion. The troops at the site ate mostly MREs (meals-ready-to-eat, the plastic-packed replacement for the old C rations). Contrary to the standing orders against giving handouts, on trips up and down the hill, the troops had been giving leftovers to the kids who lived along the road. By the time I made my first visit, the kids hounded the vehicle in packs, begging, their dirty faces pleading. Their parents often watched from the doorways of their shacks, with a look of disgust mingled with dismay at what their children had become.

At least one family, though, kept trying free enterprise. After seeing the vehicle pass by their shack on the way up, and assuming that we would shortly return, this family always had something they tried to sell us on the way down. Usually the oldest boy would come out to flag the vehicle down. He carried a paper sack that might be loaded with some pieces of chicken, but often only with tortillas.

The road to the site also provided an excellent view of one of the Honduran climates. The trees on this ridge were predominantly pine. The undergrowth contained many ferns and other wet-weather foliage. In fact, the climate up on the ridge reminded me of the climate and forests surrounding Fort Lewis, Washington. No jungle was anywhere to be found.

5 February 1986 PAB

Life is becoming more routine, boring at times. I've got the GI squirts, probably from local foods I ate over the weekend.

Went to San Lorenzo, Choluteca, Tegucigalpa, and Danli last weekend, ostensibly to check on contract operations, barge rentals for an upcoming DFT, and running power to the Grey Wolf site. In our minds (mine and Captain D's), we were on a boon-doggling adventure. We went with our .45s and a total of fourteen rounds. Quite the adventurers, huh?

The trip was magnificent, though. This country is pretty much built in strips—very regionalized, depending on the climate, the agricultural and/or the industrial base. Heading east out of Tegucigalpa, we crossed a series of valleys, each with a different climate. This was the last part of the trip and was the most uplifting part. The road was good the whole ninety-plus kilometers to Danli, and for another fifteen kilometers beyond. The primary business was agriculture, everything from coffee to pineapples. Amazingly, small farms were predominant. Most of the farms had at least one vehicle. With the exception of a few large plantations, surrounded by shacks of laborers and sharecroppers, the region was generally well off. At Rancho Jamastran, across the road from a dirt airfield the United States had built on an earlier exercise, was one of the largest and most modern houses I had ever seen.

The San Lorenzo area was a different matter. The largest town was Choluteca, with a population of about twenty thousand. It was the transshipment area for the local agriproducts, the accepted market town, and the place for the wealthy to live. A chemical plant had been built there, too. Two other towns, San Lorenzo and Nacaome, were nothing except poor mud-hut villages. Unspeakable dirt and poverty were the prevalent cultural characteristics of this area. The worst characteristic in this southern area was the plantation agriculture. The crops were cotton and watermelon, which required intensive manual labor. The laborers lived in mostly grass huts, with tile or tin roofs. Unfortunately, the average hut-dweller had far too many kids.

The geography of the south varied greatly. Volcanic and tectonic action had created a tortured landscape. Spiny ridges, cinder cones, and the volcanos of Tiger Island in Honduras's slice of the Gulf of Fonseca, and San Miguel in nearby El Salvador dominated the scenery. Huge mangrove swamps, cut only by the occasional channel and causeway, also grew in the coastal areas. Although the region was extremely dry during our visit, during the rainy reason it's the opposite. It was not uncommon to see a small sort of cactus growing next to a palm tree that was providing shade to a water-starved banana tree.

As for adventure, when we pulled into the Honduran 11th Battalion cantonment area east of San Lorenzo to check on the contract sites there, the Hondurans were on full alert. Apparently, the Nicaraguans had crossed the border several times in the preceding days. The Hondurans were prepared to retaliate on January thirty-first, but didn't get the opportunity. The Sandinistas also penetrated fifteen kilometers towards Danli while we were in that area.

On 1 February, the 1st Honduran Battalion moved into

Tegucigalpa to force Gen. Lopez Reyes, the chief of staff, to retire. The command group here went cautious and tried to consolidate all Americans. They couldn't find us because the motel we had planned to stay in was full of Grey Wolf exercise personnel.

The two motels in the south were anomalies. The Grey Wolf motel was first class in any league. The one we stayed in at Choluteca, the La Fuente, was first class but worn. The main guests at La Fuente were a group of ten to fifteen U.S. dove hunters who were proving that tourism continues despite nearby warfare. One old guy, a Citadel grad, had been coming for fifteen years.

As we ate frijoles, tortillas, and some excellent steaks in the small dining room at La Fuente, the old Citadel grad came up to talk to us. He promptly asked us if we were CIA and was pleasantly surprised to discover that we were military. He took great relish in describing the hunting trip. That particular day, the Americans had bagged over three hundred doves. The next morning, Captain D and I watched them leave for another outing. We immediately noticed that, although we were soldiers less than fifteen miles from a war zone, these tourists had us greatly outgunned. Their collection of shotguns and hunting gear would have done a guerrilla patrol proud. Our two .45s and fourteen rounds were no match. Yet this was also our last armed trip. Shortly after our return, all American personnel, except MPs, were forbidden to carry firearms off the base. The command did not want any unnecessary shooting.

The purpose of our trip had been to visit the airfield at Jamastran, a strip to be upgraded in the near future; the 11th Battalion compound where our office had contracted to have a building built, and the site of probable future work as well; and to visit the little port of Coyolito across a small neck of water from volcanic Tiger Island.

The Honduran 11th Infantry Battalion was important to the U.S. effort in Honduras for two reasons. The first was that the battalion guarded the well that supplied the water that our forces airlifted every week to the U.S. troops and technicians on Tiger Island. The second was the refueling point for the helicopters sent to supply the island. The Hondurans guarded this, too.

In an exercise conducted previously, U.S. forces had used the 11th's compound as a base camp, building several hootches and drilling the well. A few of the hootches remained. Someone had left an old truck-mounted erdalator to purify the water prior to pumping it into huge rubber bags (called blivets) for airlifting.

Captain D and I stopped in to check on a building contract. Nothing had yet been done, so we went on down to the old hootches to see the small group of American fuel handlers who looked after the erdalator and the refueling point. To my surprise, the group was about evenly split between males and females. All were dressed in civilian clothes.

I had thought that our facilities at PAB were primitive, but theirs were pathetic. The old hootches were pretty badly deteriorated, and only a couple of them had electricity. In fact, the hootch with the most electricity served as the common living area. The wiring appeared dangerously jury-rigged, but was functional enough to run a TV, VCR, and small refrigerator. The burn-out latrine (that is, a latrine where the waste is captured in half of a 55-gallon drum, to be burned periodically with a mixture of diesel) was about to fall down. Two other hootches served as separate sleeping quarters. All the buildings felt like ovens in the blistering, dry-season heat. I did not envy the detachment at all.

Not surprisingly, the young men and women gave every appearance of getting along quite well. We suspected some rather intimate relationships developed during the two-week tenures of duty. The detachment had a rental vehicle, and thus was able to shop off the local economy as well as visit the Grey Wolf unit nearby.

The Honduran conscripts surely appreciated the rather scantily clad (by Honduran standards) American girls working in their midst. Whenever the female soldiers went to check the erdalator or the fuel blivets, a crowd of young Honduran conscripts immediately appeared just to watch, never saying anything. They appeared almost transfixed by the sight, or perhaps by the very idea, of women and men soldiers cohabitating.

In comparison to the San Lorenzo detachment, the Grey Wolf troops lived very well. For some reason, the motel outside of Nacaome, a village not even deserving the appellation of "one-horse," was first-rate. It was spacious, clean, air-conditioned, and had a nice, large swimming pool. The restaurant also served excellent food, and the fare had been suitably Americanized. The American soldiers, again of mixed genders, lounged by the poolside or played Frisbee on the lawn. No one wore uniforms. The scene belonged more to southern Florida than to Honduras.

Unfortunately, for us, the whole motel was booked for the Grey Wolf contingent. Captain Dickenson and I had stopped for a room on our way to San Lorenzo, only to be turned away by the clerk. We stopped again on our way back to eat, and noticed a UH-60 Blackhawk helicopter parked on the front lawn, no more than a few feet from the building on one side and the surrounding fence on the other sides—quite a feat of flying. Upon return to Palmerola, we learned of the border crisis and the command group's worry about our condition. Evidently, the clerk was overly officious. Rooms had been available for us, but no one had told her, and she didn't ask. The Major commanding the Grey Wolf detachment told us to seek him out in the future, and he would ensure we had accommodations.

This last portion of the trip, our visit to Coyolito, proved as interesting as the rest. We left the Pan-American Highway west of Nacaome and headed south along a dirt track for several miles, alternately crossing causeways, which rose out of the swamps, and climbing hills, which afforded land dry enough for cultivation. Several small villages, little more than collections of decaying huts, were the major centers of population in the area.

Coyolito resembled the other villages with the exception of the small dock and a rather more modern structure that served as the Honduran Naval office. We parked our pickup, locking all of our baggage and our ice chest in the front. The Hondurans are a curious people, especially in the small towns and villages where foreigners are rarely seen. The people tend to cluster around such strangers and their vehicles, closely inspecting both, but saying little. We really didn't expect thievery, but didn't take any chances, either.

We approached the naval office to find some official who might become our point of contact for a forthcoming mission on Tiger Island. The mission required shipping some materials and equipment across the mile or so of water to the island. The only boat in the area apparently was a half-sunk barge belonging to the Honduran Navy.

I used my Portuguese-Spanish to ask a sailor for an officer. He took off inside, and seconds later a young Honduran of medium height and large belly came out of the building, dressed in a filthy blue uniform. I began again in my halting Spanish to explain the purpose of our visit. After a sentence or two, the young officer held up his hand for me to stop.

"Hey look, man, I speak English just fine." He did, too, without much of an accent. He had been living with an aunt in Atlanta since age twelve. He had finished high school and completed two years of college there. In reply to our questions about his presence in this backwater of Central America, he explained that two years of national service were necessary to maintain his Honduran citizenship. He had returned to his homeland, entered their Navy, and Coyolito was his assignment. Many Hondurans, he explained further, had relatives in America, and many returned to do just what he was doing. With the close proximity of the States, an industrious Honduran could have the best of both worlds.

6

DEPLOYMENTS AND EXERCISES

24 February 1986 PAB
Tomorrow we will have the following units on the ground: B Company (-), 39th Engineers; a detachment from the 287th Powerline Company, U.S. Army Reserve (USAR), from Massachusetts; a Facilities Engineer Support Agency (FESA) detachment from Fort Belvoir, Virginia; the 245 th Utilities Detachment from Fort Leavenworth, Kansas; and advanced elements from the 27th Engineer Battalion (Airborne) from Fort Bragg, North Carolina.

Engineer activities in CENTAM have figured prominently in the Washington Post and other Eastern papers recently. All the articles insinuate scandal and underhanded dealings by the nasty ol' military. As one who works in the office that regulates, contracts for, and oversees most of the Honduran construction activities (primarily those at PAB, which interest congressmen most), I can state authoritatively that nearly everything that we are accused of hiding is available in at least half a dozen offices. Most of the projects are not classified except for dates and exact locations. We go to painstaking lengths to notify our higher-ups of projects, and they pass it on. Brigadier General Schroeder, deputy chief of engineers for facility engineering, was here recently. We cleared up many of his misperceptions so that he could adequately brief Congress.

The problem lies in media-created hysteria, ignorance of contracting and budgeting procedures, ignorance of the chains of command, and inadequate filing systems. A large contributing factor is the turnover in personnel, with the attendant short institutional memory. No doubt we contribute to the problem when we do construction by troops or contract that contravenes regulations. However, most of that contravention is through ignorance of the many regulations or through sheer inexperience. Even in those cases, we go to pains to get the results annotated to the master plan of Palmerola kept at Howard AFB in Panama.

I was the senior Army engineer at Palmerola. My position as the joint staff engineer for the task force made me the principal engineer advisor to the task force commander on all engineer matters, at least theoretically. I had graduated from the engineer officer basic course less than a year before my arrival. That course gives only the rudimentary how-to skills needed by lieutenants to lead work crews for vertical and horizontal construction. It did not teach much about the design of base camps, electrical distribution systems, water systems, or pavements. All those subjects are taught in the engineer officer advanced course. Nor did I have enough applied engineering at West Point to adequately solve heavy-duty civil-engineering problems. Fortunately, Captain D had both the necessary education and the experience. Unfortunately, Captain D, an Air Force officer, was at times baffled by Army paperwork requirements.

Captain D and I evolved into a capable team. He spent much of his time working on designs, aided by the other two skilled USAF engineer officers who eventually came to work in the office. The Lieutenant and I spent the bulk of our time planning and providing engineering supplies and equipment for the small-unit deployments for training (called DFTs usually, but sometimes deployment training exercises, DTEs), rebuilding bunkers, classifying bridges, seeing to the engineering needs (sanitation, water, floors for tents, construction materials and equipment, etc.) of the larger exercise groups that used Palmerola, and identifying possible future projects. The NCOs of both services in our office busied themselves with handling the hundreds of thousands of dollars' worth of construction supplies and tools that we ordered, received, and distributed.

Eventually, the work lines divided our responsibilities into nearly distinct areas. The USAF engineers worked largely on contracting for Palmerola Air Base, and the Army engineers worked the deployment projects. As the USAF commander explained to us near the end of my tour, the de facto division we created closely approximated the one intended by the manning document, but until late February 1986, there had never been enough engineers to operate as designed.

Still, we did not function fully in the political environment of our projects. Seemingly innocent construction could easily be blown out of proportion in the press. Convert a few of the crumbling huts to beer joints, and it would be insinuated that we had come to stay, that we were on the incremental road to another Vietnam. Build a market road, and some reporter would see it as a covert plot to aid the Contras, even if the road was a hundred miles west of the Contra zone. Yet we did our best to keep our superiors informed, and they, in turn, kept theirs informed up the chain all the way to Congress. Maybe the fact that so much of what we were doing in Honduras was so innocuous, that reporters, politicians, and even common citizens, who had been fed a daily diet for twenty years of American soldier as the bad guy and the American government as a factory of lies, had to assume more sinister motives and actions.

The Engineer units on the ground in late February 1986 were examples of so much of what was good in   the Army of the mid-1980s— and some of the bad, too.

B Company (-) of the 39th Engineer Battalion (Combat), Fort Devens, Massachusetts, had arrived in late January. They were the first DFT unit I worked with. The company deployed in two giant C-5A cargo aircraft with a minimum complement of equipment—just enough to do the job—and only about 75 troops, out of the perhaps 120 total in the company. The rest had stayed behind.

B Company worked on three projects. Two were of great importance to Palmerola, and the other was an experimental project linked to antiterrorism. The first project was the construction of a forty-eight-foot timber- trestle bridge with a military load class of 60 (Bridges are classified by the vehicle weight they are designed to carry and by how the weight is distributed over the wheelbase or, in the case of armored vehicles, over the tracks. A class 60 bridge could support a medium tank). This bridge crossed the little creek running through the base. An old, narrow concrete bridge of extremely low weight class existed, but could not support the traffic load of an expanded Palmerola. The new bridge was intended to link up any new expansion of the base on the far shore of the creek. Additionally, a planned, or rather hoped-for, ammo dump was to be built in the fields across the creek.

B Company was composed mainly of combat engineers, who were basically infantrymen with rudimentary construction skills. The bridge they built was not pretty, but it was sturdy and functional. However, the design called for bents (trestles built on wooden footings) rather than piles, which meant the design life was six months to a year. As the amount of precipitation that would fall in the rainy season was unknown, we wondered if the bridge would make it through the first wet season. In the meantime, the new access increased the traffic across the creek many times over.

The other major project B Company worked on was the construction of a 126,000-gallon water tank. The tank was sorely needed to combat the water shortages caused by the frequent power outages. Again, the combat engineers went to work, using hand ratchets to tighten the thousands of bolts that held the steel plates together. As no scaffolding was available, the engineers worked off the headache racks of five-ton dump trucks. Unfortunately, the combat engineers had neither the tools nor the training necessary to hook the tank into our existing water system. Moreover, the tank was from war stocks, and the insides of its panels were so rusty that they needed sandblasting. The crates it arrived in had been originally stenciled with an address in the former Republic of Vietnam.

The final mission of B Company was to be the construction of a ballistic berm—basically a wall made of a synthetic fabric stretched over a wooden frame then filled with tamped sand. Originally, the berm was intended to protect the field hospital which was located only a hundred meters or so from the main north-south road linking San Pedro Sula and Tegucigalpa. Unfortunately, not enough of the material was sent to do that job properly, so the berm was built around the water towers and showers in the middle of the base. The military wanted to see how the berm would hold up in a tropical environment. Posts were sunk in the ground. A simple wooden frame was built on the posts, and the fabric was stretched over the frame. Sand was dumped into the fabric from the bucket of a John Deere 410 backhoe and then tamped. As the berm was in the middle of the base, its durability was tested by the climate, but it served no actual antiterrorist function.

One detachment of B Company got the opportunity to perform a last mission. The command group informed the engineer office one day that a dirt strip near Puerto Lempira in Honduran Miskitia had been damaged by recent rains. The strip needed upgrading before a unit of the Arkansas National Guard could be extracted. The mission was "immediate" as the guardsmen's two-week tour of duty was nearing an end. A quick crisis-planning session ascertained that the Engineer forces would have to come from either B Company, or from Task Force 135 of the Missouri National Guard, which was working on the market road in the Yoro Valley in the north.

To do the job, the planning cell anticipated that all that was necessary was to grade the strip and, perhaps, re- compact the surface. The grading and compacting equipment would have to be loaded onto a relatively small C-130 aircraft to get to the field. However, no one at Palmerola had the necessary expertise to strip the roll-over protection (the metal cage that protects the operator) from a road grader. After some thought, someone came up with the idea of contacting the Airborne Engineers at Fort Bragg. I called the S3 shop (the Operations section) of the 20th Engineer Brigade there, which quickly gave us the information needed. Task Force 135 agreed to provide the grader, and B Company, 39th provided the manpower, a pickup truck, and a towed vibratory roller.

A second lieutenant was dispatched with a small detachment to do the job. The J6 (signal section) attached a communication team with satellite capability, and the USAF sent a team to verify the safety of the repaired runway. Amazingly, this whole operation was concocted in three or four days, with only minimal wrangling between the Army and the Air Force, and among Palmerola, SOUTHCOM (Southern Command, the unified command responsible for U.S. actions in Latin America), and FORSCOM (the command responsible for seeing to the training and regulating of active and reserve component Army and National Guard units in the continental United States). The young platoon leader seemed bewildered at first by the rather sketchy details of his mission, but he accomplished the mission with alacrity. The Arkansas Guard made it home on time.

We had several other units on the ground. The 245th Utilities Detachment came from Fort Leavenworth. The Facilities Engineer Support Agency (FESA) detachment came primarily from Fort Belvoir, Virginia, but some of its men also came from Fort Bliss, Texas. The 287th

Powerline Company was a U.S. Army Reserve unit out of Massachusetts. All of them were at Palmerola to do electrical upgrades.

PAB was a camp built out of wood, tin, screen, and canvas, and thus was extremely vulnerable to fire. The generally shoddy wiring done by Honduran contractors exacerbated the potential for fire. The American soldiers and airmen didn't help the problem by modifying the wiring whenever they could. Each hootch had two circuits, one for lighting and the other for appliances. It was not unusual to find double the allowable number of receptacles in some hootches, the residents having installed the additional ones. The hospital was the worst. It seemed that the nurses were especially attracted to anyone who might claim to have been an electrician as a civilian or to have wired his own house or a hunting cabin. One nurse's hootch did catch fire from the sheer number of appliances plugged into its overloaded twenty- amp circuit.

Consequently, upgrading the electrical wiring was always near the top of our agenda. I have already described the problem with power outages. The only solution was to have U.S. troops rewire the base to American National Electric Code standards. The problem with that idea was the paucity of trained exterior electricians. Hence, the necessity of bringing in the Reserves.

The half-dozen Reserve NCOs of the 287th who came down were highline workers as civilians. They were experts at their jobs. In fact, they gave up quite a bit of overtime pay to spend a week in Honduras as an ice storm hit New England and busted a lot of lines. The FESA troops were all experts at power supply and distribution, too. Most were senior NCOs, but one very talented captain came as well to command the effort. These experts immediately discovered that the Hondurans had wired up the transformers on most of Palmerola in the wrong configuration, thus reducing the possible power by as much as two-thirds and causing the numerous outages. In a matter of days, the two groups of experts had most of the serious problems corrected.

The wartime mission of the 245th was to maintain a base camp, so its deployment to PAB was considered prime training. They came to rewire a few dozen hootches belonging to the 224th Military Intelligence Battalion. The FESA soldiers again provided the technical oversight and quality control for the project. The 245th also utilized its carpenters to fix numerous annoying problems around the compound and at the small installation on top of Tiger Island. We would have liked to have made the 245th a permanent fixture on Palmerola.

One of the conversations I had with SOUTHCOM during these deployments concerned units like the 245th. My question was why one of these units couldn't be assigned for a few months to the base on a rotating basis. Unsurprisingly, the answer had to do with politics. For such a unit to deploy just to maintain Palmerola would smack of operations rather than training. Operations were not allowed. The fiction that the military maintained was that all troops in Honduras were there just for training. In the collective political mind, the very word operations evidently smacked of war.

Moreover, all deployments had to be properly forecasted, funded, and accounted for, and that took months of lead-time. The Army could not afford to deploy engineers just to do work as it came up. All work had to be planned far in advance. Naturally, to anyone faced with trying to keep the camp functional, such explanations seemed mighty weak. My suggestion was that the Army should send a utilities detachment to Palmerola on a long ARTEP (an Army Readiness, Training, and Evaluation Program) to see how well they had been trained for their wartime missions. Of course, during the ARTEP, that unit would also solve many of my headaches. SOUTHCOM and FORSCOM let me know unequivocally that the funding and auditing bureaucrats would never buy such a levelheaded suggestion.

The advance party of the 27th Engineer Battalion (Airborne) arrived to establish a support operation for Cabanas '86, a contingency exercise. The 27th's part in the exercise was to build a C-130-capable dirt strip in the vicinity of Mocoron in the Honduran northeast, an area inaccessible by road. The majority of the battalion and its equipment were to parachute into the area, build the strip, and then be airlifted out. Later in the dry season, the 2d Battalion of the 75th Rangers was to assault the strip in a practice exercise, and afterwards conduct joint patrolling exercises with the local Honduran infantry units. A small detachment of carpenters was to be sent by helicopter to an equally remote place south of Mocoron to help some villagers build a schoolhouse.

Because of the remoteness of these projects, our office had to do extra work. The base camp that the 27th established in Mocoron required thousands of board feet of lumber. PAB had to contract for the lumber from local sawmills. When they could not supply all that we needed, we procured other lumber in the vicinity of PAB and airlifted it out. The schoolhouse project required a small cement mixer. Odd as it may seem, the equipment authorization of the 27th did not include small mixers. We scoured the local rental markets for one. Eventually we found one, rented it, and then helicoptered it out to the remote site, too.

The 27th was undoubtedly the finest engineer unit I had seen. Other units experienced a few problems operating in the Central American theater. Two soldiers from B Company, 39th went absent without leave (AWOL) while in Honduras. They were eventually tracked down in San Pedro Sula. The tale associated with their disappearance was lurid in every respect. The two supposedly had intended to fake the death of one of them, so that his girlfriend, purportedly a colonel's daughter back in Massachusetts, could collect his serviceman's life insurance. They had hoped to do this by murdering a Honduran, chopping his head off, and burning the body with American dog tags attached. Then, all three planned a reunion in Rio.

The other problem I observed also concerned a deployed engineer unit and was all too typical of life at Palmerola. One night just before its departure, I went to visit them in the tent city where we housed DFT units. The tents were pitched across the road from the JTFB hospital club, The Recovery Room. I went in the commander's tent, and found him and his senior lieutenant talking to a rather attractive female. She turned out to be a Reserve nurse who had just finished her two-week annual training requirement. She and the commander were seated embarrassingly close, fawning over one another. Only a couple of weeks before, he had been showing me pictures of his wife and kids. Upon returning to his home base, he subsequently dumped his wife in favor of the nurse and was relieved of his command.

Morality, or the absence of it—or maybe we should call the subject modern values—was a problem at Palmerola, at least in my opinion. Many of us were married. Naturally, we missed our families, but after a while, infidelity reared its ugly head. Talk of sex was constant. Some of the

71

married guys visited the Zona Roja in nearby Comayagua. The zone catered to two classes of clientele—those of modest means, and those with hardly any. The former were generally Americans, and rumor had it they were serviced by true professionals who had trekked to Comayagua from the oil fields in Venezuela. The latter clients were mainly Hondurans, but also GIs near the end of the month. Those with little money had to go to "Ten Limp Alley," a street in the Zona named after the standard charge— ten lempira, or five dollars. The alley predated our arrival by decades.

If Zona Roja was out of the question, as it was for the female soldiers, then one could take up with another service member. The Recovery Room was the most popular place on base because it had the largest supply of females, married or otherwise. The bunkers became a favorite place for the clandestine liaisons. R & R trips to one of the few good hotels in the country provided other opportunities.

As an example, one married field-grade officer, a man, struck up quite a relationship with one of the field-grade women. Maybe the relationship was entirely innocent, but he spent enough off-duty time with her to cause even the other senior officers to comment on the fact among themselves. I passed his hootch one night at 0300 on my way to the latrine as she was coming out to smoke a cigarette on his steps, clad only in a sheer nightgown. On my way back she was gone. Did the senior officers have to be puritans? Certainly not, but some should have been more discreet about their own behavior.

Occasionally, someone would bring up the subject of marital fidelity. This usually brought forth lots of elbow nudging, winking, and chuckling. Eventually someone else would provide the inevitable answer, "Well, I'm not married in Honduras, only in the States!" followed by more nudging, winking, and chuckling.

In the early 1980s, the Army began to move away from the use of alcohol as a social lubricant. Under guidance from the Army leadership, base commanders terminated "happy hours" at the on-base clubs. The Stateside drinking age was raised to twenty-one. NCO and officers clubs adopted atmospheres revolving around dining and family activities. Soon, the clubs had all the ambience of a Western Sizzler or Bonanza steakhouse, but with worse service and food; consequently, they became less popular. At Palmerola, though, alcohol was still king. It was the common form of recreation, usually in the form of beer.

Palmerola was blessed with drinking clubs. Every major unit on base had at least one close by. The 11th Signal Brigade (Forward) had sited its club between the task force headquarters and its own billets. The Pink Pig and The Cockpit belonged to the 224th MI Battalion. The notorious Recovery Room belonged to the hospital. The aviation and logistical sections had perhaps the largest and poshest club, across the runway at Camp Blackjack, two crumbling hootches joined by a covered breezeway, and someone had installed a wide-screen TV. As PAB's post exchange sold no hard liquor, the clubs specialized in beer marked up about a nickel per can or bottle. The profits went toward unit parties or, rumor had it, purchase of satellite dishes.

For a change, servicemen could go to town to drink the local beer. Honduras produced three relatively good beers. The most common and the cheapest were Imperial and Nacional, light lagers selling for little more than a quarter a bottle. Port Royal was produced in the banana belt in the north. Its labels were printed in English, as it was intended for export. Port Royal closely resembled imported European lagers in taste and price (about $1.50 per bottle). A night on the town was a cheap drunk if you stuck to the first two.

Hard liquor was tough to come by. Honduras produced Flor de Caña, a dark rum, selling for a couple of dollars per liter. Few Americans developed a taste for it. Most got their liquor from the lucky few who went TDY Stateside or to Panama. Such individuals left with hefty liquor orders that presented problems of packing and Customs clearance upon return. Some of us had contacts either in the MILGROUP or at the embassy in the capital and could arrange a purchase through the exchange there. Possession of liquor bestowed a certain status and popularity. Hence, even those who didn't drink often availed themselves of opportunities to buy.

Given the availability of alcohol, it's surprising that it didn't cause more problems. Few soldiers at PAB, though, had access to vehicles. One only had to walk a few yards to get to a club. Buses ran into Comayagua for extracurricular drinking. The long working hours and the dearth of hard liquor also militated against problem drinking. Nonetheless, alcohol was too easily seen as a prime factor of morale. The condition might best be summed up in the words of an engineer captain's after- action report covering his unit's deployment. "The environment at Palmerola Air Base seems to promote the heavy consumption of alcohol. Several clubs are open and selling beer to service members every evening at Palmerola. Since recreational opportunities in the evening are limited, the clubs do a brisk business. Also, large quantities of beer are sold at the base exchange. The atmosphere at Palmerola does not seem to be in keeping with the Army's policies to deglamorize alcohol."[24]

Most of the activities going on in Honduras at any time were engineering or medical related. The medical activities were of enormous importance to improving the quality of life for the Hondurans. Medical personnel in the military, along with the finance, public affairs, and JAG personnel, were generally derided by junior soldiers and junior officers as being only civilians in uniform, collecting a paycheck. But in Honduras they served as a key ingredient in American policy. They did their jobs by running the hospital—a jumble of tents and shacks—at PAB, holding clinics every Thursday at the front gate of the base for the surrounding population, and by going out on medical readiness training exercises (MEDRETEs).

The deployment of a MEDRETE was quite a sight. Early in the morning, a trickle of vehicles of all kinds would snake from the hospital on the main side of PAB around the north end of the runway to Camp Blackjack. Medics, nurses, dentists, and doctors clung to the vehicles with their kits. They were clad in all manner of uniforms befitting an insufficiently militarized force: boonie hats, fatigue caps, colored scarves, some with Army-issue gear, and some with civilian gear.

A cloud of dust signaled the arrival of the convoy at the helicopter flight line. There, the force and its equipment would load onto helicopters to be transported to some remote village. The medics took along MREs and jugs of chlorinated water for lunch and dinner. Once deployed, they spent the day treating whatever came their way, human or animal. They gave instruction in basic health and hygiene to anyone who would listen. Immunizations and pulled teeth must have numbered in the many thousands over the space of a few months. For villagers with serious conditions, the teams arranged care, either at PAB or the nearest Honduran facility. Sometimes, due to the lack of communications, the villages didn't even know the teams were coming. However, word spread quickly once the helicopters landed, and the medics always had a crowd. However lighthearted the members were on their departure, at the end of the day, the MEDRETE team would arrive back at the base dirty, tired, thirsty, and hungry. They would climb slowly into their assortment of borrowed, overloaded vehicles and head slowly around the dusty perimeter road back to the hospital, truly the unsung heroes of America's efforts in Central America.

9 March 1986 PAB

A lot has passed in the last eight days. On March 1st I spent most of the day conversing in Spanish (or my Portuguese version of it) with Mr. Reyes and the Lieutenant Colonel serving as the Army Forces Commander (ARFOR) in Honduras. Mr. Reyes owns the ranch on which our TACAN site was built. Mr. Reyes wanted the road to the TACAN site fixed as partial payment of the rent for the site.

Hondurans still believed in gentlemen's agreements. They also believed that the bounty of America's involvement was unfettered and endless. During the negotiations for the TACAN site, someone had given Mr. Reyes to understand that his road would be fixed as part of the bargain. There was nothing in writing to that effect, but he was convinced of the "deal's" efficacy, nonetheless. He was a lawyer, so he knew that the only card he could play was to increase his demands formally when the current contract ran out. Of course, we had to have the site. Similar problems arose with the city officials of Comayagua.

From time to time, the mayor would demand that we pave some of its streets in return for our recreational use of the town. Chlorinating the city water supply was another scheme on which a study was done. However worthy these projects would have been as civic action, they were expensive and exceeded our military engineering capabilities. We could not get the funding, equipment, and troops even to pave the roads on the air base. The Hondurans assumed selfish duplicity on our part and refused to understand the legalities of congressional authorizations, contracting procedures, and the use of troop labor for non-training missions. The officials also did not want to buy the idea that the GI cash that flowed to the restaurants, bars, discos, whorehouses, and construction firms was compensation enough for the disruption we caused them.

9 March 1986 PAB
What was really interesting, though, were Mr. Reyes's views on Central America. He's a lawyer in Comayaguela—*a member of Honduras' upper middle class. His wife had worked extensively for USAID, the U.S. MILGROUP, and other U.S. agencies. He thought Carter had been a bad president for the United States, and very bad for Central and Latin America. He seemed to mean that Carter's rhetoric and policies on human rights had tied the hands of Latin governments in dealing with subversives. He definitely meant that Carter had erred in allowing and aiding the Sandinistas to come to power, especially when the Sandinistas turned left. Mr. Reyes also had harsh words for today's liberals who seek to throttle the defense against Sandinista and Cuban subversion. He knew that America would suffer if Central America suffered. He said that diplomacy was not enough, as could be seen with our past dealings with several communist regimes.*

This was a very picturesque scene: two U.S. Army officers in jungle fatigues sipping coffee on the veranda of a mountain cottage. Our host and hostess were most gracious. In fact they were so gracious that I must admit I wondered whether we would have been treated better or worse had we not been Americans. They brought out several cups of steaming, strong Honduran coffee and a platter of small sugar cookies. Our conversation wound between Mr. Reyes's concerns about his new road, and the general geopolitics of Central America. While we sat there on top of his mountain, clouds rolled across Mr. Reyes's lawn. Mr. Reyes also tried to interest us in his mountain spring as a water supply for the TACAN site. Remembering how we had gotten ourselves into the mess over the road, we made it a point not to say much at all.

9 March 1986 PAB
I then went on a TDY trip with two Air National Guard lieutenant colonels to inspect possible construction at Cerro La Mole. When the Sandinistas violate the border, it is said that the muzzle flashes can

be seen from here. These nation-assistance and security projects would be in jeopardy if the liberals get their way—too threatening to the Nicaraguans I suppose.

The Air National Guard had pilots who regularly flew into Honduras in support of U.S. activities. Now there was a move to involve the Air Guard's considerable engineering assets. As we were always short of engineers, this move was welcome, and PAB looked forward to their arrival in May. SOUTHCOM wanted to assign to the Air Guard the mission of erecting a radar dome at Cerro La Mole. PAB also had several small buildings that we wanted constructed or refurbished.

The lieutenant colonels and I discussed billeting and messing arrangements with the contract employees who ran and maintained the equipment at Cerro La Mole. This was a plush site compared to PAB. It consisted of several large containerized vans stationed on top of a mound of earth. The civilian employees worked in shifts. They spent several twenty-four-hour days on site, followed by a few days off in Tegucigalpa, where some had stationed their families. While on the site, they lived in small trailer houses. They had all the electricity, refrigeration, and hot water they needed—these people knew how to deploy to remote areas.

A squad of Air Force security police was also stationed there. However, the real security came from a large detachment of Honduran soldiers. As this was close to the border, security was serious business. The site was surrounded by fenced-off minefields. Around the containers, the Hondurans had also fixed ancient antiaircraft guns, which appeared to be forty-millimeters. The guns were trained in the direction of Nicaragua. Yet, given the age of the cannon and the average training of the Honduran troops, I'd have given the advantage to any of the Soviet-supplied gunships that might have crossed the border.

The Air National Guard officers and I did what surveying we needed so that their units could start their planning. We then returned to Tegucigalpa, where they caught flights back to the United States.

9 March 1986 PAB
Next, I went to San Pedro Sula and the ruins of Copan, both in the north of the country. This area was wealthier by far: three times the per capita

income of the rest of the nation due to the banana business. The wealth was reflected in the life-styles, vehicles, appliances, homes. The farms were bigger, so were the ranches and plantations. Parts looked like Pennsylvania or Georgia. San Pedro itself could have been in Europe. Land was fairly well distributed. This area will be hard to socialize or communize.

Copan's ruins need developing. There were too many kids and too few schools.

The trip to San Pedro Sula was a "morale, welfare, and recreation" (MWR) trip. Transportation and lodging were provided courtesy of Uncle Sam. It was, in all senses of the term, a boondoggle. I went with the commander of the 245th Utilities Detachment, a friend who had graduated a year ahead of me at West Point. We stayed in the Copantl Sul Hotel, the equal of the Maya in Tegucigalpa. Between journalists, soldiers, and government employees, Americans were a common sight at the Maya, but that was not the case at the Copantl. We stuck out like dusty, shabbily dressed, sore thumbs.

Worse, the hotel was hosting a gathering of Latin American legislators. They and their ladies were decked out in their finery. Here was a fine contrast: Latin legislators, renowned for their anti-Yankee sentiments, having to rub elbows with American soldiers— refined members of South America's elite classes crammed into the same accommodations with the grubby tools that kept them in power. I don't mean this as a left-wing critique. The exact same attitude, one of sniffing, snorting, the witty political barb or comment on fashion, the disdain for lower classes (especially soldiers), and the contemptuous looks down long noses from heads tilted skyward are just as openly on display at any Army-Harvard football game.

My colleague and I spent one night in a bar in San Pedro that had a reputation for being the place where mercenaries hung out. The place was as nondescript as any other. We went in and found that it was run by an expatriate American. There was no crowd—certainly no loud, hard-drinking mercs—only a few Hondurans. The American woman behind the bar served us drinks for a couple of hours as we played board games that she kept below the bar. Board games! So much for the steely killer types. The only thing that might have suggested that the establishment was a merc bar was the bill she gave us at the end. We had been buying four-dollar drinks without knowing it, a virtual fortune in Honduras, where beer can be as cheap as a quarter. In barracks parlance, we had been f**ked without even being kissed. Only mercenaries, making their legendary salaries, or extremely well-heeled natives could have afforded to drink there.

9 March 1986 PAB

One last observation—I've noticed it ever since I've been here, but it didn't click in my mind. Most of the houses and shacks down here are still flying the flags of their presidential candidate. What seems wonderfully democratic and bodes well for the future of Honduras is that no candidate appeared to have controlled a bloc vote. Most houses flew different flags. Rarely did I see more than a dozen homes together with the same flag. Thus, the electorate has yet to be split into classes or regional blocs.

Another note: family-planning clinics are in several locales I've passed through. Condoms are prominent in drug stores. Near San Pedro, I even saw a gigantic billboard advertising condoms. Pretty amazing for a supposedly backward Catholic country.

10 March 1986 PAB

The JTFB Commander gave a good speech last night at the farewell for the acting first sergeant. He said we could hear a helicopter, if we listened, that was carrying a six-year-old boy with a heart problem to Tegucigalpa. Without us being here, the boy would have died. The other helicopters and planes we had been hearing all day, he said, were ferrying troops and equipment to emphasize that we are determined to aid a society seeking a representative system. We had a vague notion of it, he stated, but emphasized that we were not hearing choppers carrying wounded, or planes carrying coffins. We were trying to win "smart" down here, "not like the last time!" I hadn't though much of him before, but he raised himself a notch tonight in my eyes, but only a notch.

16 March 1986 PAB
What a hectic week! Captain D was sick in bed all week with a stomach virus. Ahuas Tara (AT) '86 was coming in. We had nearly seventy-two hours without water. Sporadic power outages. I got my ass munched several times over the hooking up and sandblasting of the new water tank. That's not my job, but luckily Captain D had most of it done already.

One senior officer was a thin, tall man with a perpetually red face. He was an infantry officer who had previously been in the SOUTHCOM J3 (the operations officer). That job should have provided him with the experience and sensitivity to be a superb participant in the U.S. effort in Honduras. Yet, he was a man who could not recognize, let alone transcend, his shortcomings.

Despite his extensive experience in Central America and his fluency in Spanish, he did not respect the locals. Granted, the officer spent most of his time hobnobbing with the elite that composed the general staff and the political class in the capital. Perhaps this colored his view of the rest of the Hondurans. Often he saw the locals as being little more than hindrances on the road to his and the unit's success.

How did such an attitude manifest itself? Whenever we had problems with the power, the Engineers would have to brief him on the situation. One of his stock responses was that if the local official gave us any trouble about restoring power, just come to him, and he would give us a bottle of expensive Scotch whiskey to use as a bribe.

On another occasion, Harbert was ordered to spray the dirt road around the airfield with waste oil to cut down the dust. This was a direct violation of U.S. environmental law and service regulations. Fortunately, one of our NCOs saw the Harbert truck in the act and stopped it. That prompted a heated call from the red-faced officer to us. It seems he had worked a deal with the local Harbert director over a few drinks the evening before. We had no doubt that the Harbert engineers knew the law, but their contract was up for renewal, so they were willing to satisfy the whims of the senior officers. Our office went to great lengths to explain the law and regulations.

"Jesus, sir, you just can't use waste oil or any other petroleum products as a dust palliative. It's against the law and destructive of the environment."

"But this ain't America, Captain. It's Honduras, and I'm sure they wouldn't mind a little less dust either. It affects their planes just like it does ours. Harbert said it wouldn't be any problem," would be the reply.

"But, sir, we are bound by the law and service regulations wherever we serve, whether it's Honduras, Europe, or the States. Harbert knows damn good and well that they're not supposed to be doing this."

"All right! Then you damn engineers get me a goddamn dust suppressant that is legal."

The thought that we might be trashing the Honduran environment or treating the locals as inferior to Americans when it came to living standards must not have crossed his mind. The little Honduran settlement that had grown up outside the compound relied on the stream that the 39th Engineers had just put the bridge over for its drinking and washing water. When the rains came, the runoff from any oil placed on the roads would have fouled the creek.

The American effort did not need to deal with any self- generated problems of this sort. The experience of most of the senior officers should have clued them into this. Yet, some continued to cut back-channel deals with officials. Several of our engineering problems came from their vague promises to the local officials concerning paving streets, chlorinating water supplies, even to inspecting and trying to fix a leaking dam. When we could not possibly deliver on the promises, the Americans looked bad to the Hondurans, and the Engineers looked like idiots to everyone else.

Another senior officer was infected with what might be called a GI attitude. It was a mixture of bravado, bluster, and hard-driving—a caricature composed of parts from many characters in war films and novels. Indeed, at times it seemed as if he were playing a part according to a script only he knew. He was quite competent in most tactical matters. He understood the general reasons why we were in Honduras. Despite his failings, he even had a sense of the good that could come from our presence and was committed to it. Yet his GI attitude led him to mistake and misplace compassion and understanding for leadership on too many occasions.

This officer's idea of the GI at play was Hollywood's. The American soldier in his world was one who drank hard and chased members of the opposite sex. Consequently, we had the large number of clubs at PAB. Additionally, several times an hour, a bus left to take GIs down to Comayagua for the diversions there. Supposedly, a GI could only go to town twice a week, but nobody checked. Even when the terrorist threat-level was high, the buses rolled. The bus schedule violated several of the antiterrorist rules: it was a large, easily identified target moving at regular intervals along an isolated path. It was full of Americans. That no terrorist ever hit the buses with an ambush says more about the incompetence of the local left-wing organizations than it does about the wisdom of the liberty policy (but see Appendix A).

The liberty policy also allowed anyone in country for 90 days to take one free R & R trip, and anyone with a 180-day tour to take two. These trips were arranged and paid for through the Morale, Welfare, and Recreation Office, which was run by a civilian sent to PAB from the States. Imagine it. The rigors of being in country for a whole ninety days entitled you to a free trip to a resort hotel, Mayan ruins, a beach—you name it. The duty may have been uncomfortable but it was not tough. Later in my tour, I was to see this policy taken to an absurd length.

Yet, to give the senior officers credit, some led by example. It was not unusual to see one of them toting his bottle of Scotch off to one of the clubs, or hosting visiting dignitaries to a booze-soaked barbecue under the bohio. The guests always included the ubiquitous Harbert director, in search of his new contract.

Complementing the GI attitude was the combat-arms mentality. This mentality is most prevalent among Infantry and Armor officers. It requires them to demand that combat-support or service-support officers accomplish their orders to the letter. If the supporting officers raise objections based on feasibility, legality, or good sense, the combat-arms mentality requires that the order then be shouted. If the shouting does not rattle the supporting officers out of their recalcitrant stupidity, then the orders must be shouted again, this time accompanied by a few disparaging comments of a personal or professional nature.

Many—maybe even most, but certainly the best— senior combat-arms officers are those who seek to understand the constraints placed on the "tail" portion of the Army that supports the "teeth." It is precisely the "tail" that is so important in nation-building operations that are used to prevent an insurgency. The best officers have an attitude created from years of listening to their Intelligence, Supply, Signal, Civil Affairs, Medical, and Engineer staff officers. Often, their experience comes with formal civilian education in a related field, or from having served in such positions themselves. But, the bull-headed, loudmouthed variety also exists. These few bad ones overshadow the many good. The water-tank incident serves as a good illustration. The incident happened at the daily staff meeting.

"Where's Captain D?" one of the colonels asked when the Engineer portion of the brief came around.

"Sir, he's got quarters because of an acute stomach virus," I replied.

"When's the new water tank going to be operational?"

"Sir, according to SOUTHCOM, we can't hook the water tank up until the rust on the inside has been sand- blasted off. The designs for the hookup and distribution system also have to be completed and a contract let for the construction."

This must have been the tenth time such information had been given to the commander himself, his two deputies, and many of the rest at the briefing.

"Look, I gave specific instructions to Captain D that I wanted that goddamn tank fixed, and fixed now. Going without water every time the power shuts down is bullshit! I don't know why the hell you people built the damn tank if you weren't going to use it!"

"But sir, nothing can be done until a contract is let for the sandblasting, and that is going to cost money that SOUTHCOM says we don't have yet. Captain D is almost through with the plans for the hookup, but he's down sick ..." was my lame rebuttal.

"Look, Captain," the colonel interrupted with a distinct punctuation that filled me with dread. "I am tired of fucking excuses. You call Panama and tell them that I want the tank sandblasted. There aren't too many people down there who outrank me, and I want this finished. As for the plans, I want your office to have them on my desk by the end of the day. Do you understand me?"

"Yes sir!"

This exchange took place in a packed briefing room in front of other officers and NCOs. Although to the uninitiated, such an exchange between a senior and a subordinate may not seem serious; in the small, close-knit group we had become, this dressing-down was a particular embarrassment to me. I was sure that most of the sweaty, smelly, unwashed people in the room were going to blame me personally for their condition. Without proper authorizations, equipment, or personnel, and without funds, an Engineer can accomplish little. Our office had none of these with which to solve the water problem, but some in the taskforce leadership apparently chose to believe that we were either incompetent or that we actually reveled in the misery the lack of water caused.

The exchange also pointed out a deficiency in perspective that many in Palmerola originally shared. Captain D and I had labored to correct this perspective with a fair degree of success among the senior officers in that briefing room, with the exception of the commander. Everyone knows that most people in the medical corps have a specialty, and one would not ask an orthopedic surgeon for advice on a heart condition. Likewise, one would not order an aviator to take off in a plane or a helicopter without first asking whether he was qualified on the aircraft. The engineering profession is similar. Army Engineers may have an education in civil, mechanical, electrical, hydrological, or any other engineering specialty. Or, they may be trained as historians or journalists—or in any other "soft" discipline—but serve as combat engineer officers responsible for supporting Infantry or Armor operations through the construction or destruction of minefields, obstacles, and fighting positions—activities that do not require extensive technical knowledge. These latter officers, of whom I was one, only receive rudimentary training by the Army in heavy- duty engineering. Captain D was a USAF engineer, and the Air Force normally required civil engineering training as a qualification. The trick was to put appropriately trained engineers in the right spots. Unfortunately, the Army all too often tries to maintain the fiction that anyone wearing the Engineer insignia on his collar is suited for any Engineer mission. We had trained most people on PAB to understand that before grandiose demands made on the engineer office could be expected to be accomplished, the correct engineering resources, human and material, had to be applied to the problem.[1] The combat-arms mentality never accepted this.

I left the briefing room with the order of calling up the Engineer lieutenant colonels in Panama to "order" them to fix our water tank. They laughed, but said they would call the colonel to try and make him understand. My next stop was to see Captain D. I woke him up. He looked pale and nauseous. I told him that he had to finish the hookup plans by COB (close of business) that afternoon. He laughed, too. He said that the plans were so involved that he couldn't finish them in that amount of time even if he were well. His next move was to call the JTFB Air Force Commander (the AFFOR) to explain the situation one more time. Meanwhile, the power came back on, the existing water tank refilled, the flush toilets began working, and the demands were forgotten until the next power outage.

Poor leadership style led to a particularly poignant episode on the last night of my tour. About 2300 hours, the JTFB JAG officer—a military lawyer—who had moved into our hootch, burst in to get some paperwork. He was livid.

"The bastard's gone too far this time!" he shouted.

"What are you talking about?" someone asked.

"This idiot is going to give a field-grade Article 15 to an MP who stopped him at the gate. He can't do that. The kid was only doing his job. The colonel's been drinking, and he's pissed that the kid on guard didn't recognize him. Now he's going to ruin the kid's career by giving him an Article 15 for insubordination. I'm going to see if I can stop him. If I can't, I'm going to report him somewhere."

The officer, one of the field-grade commanders, had been downtown eating and drinking with some American civilians. He was in civilian clothes. When they pulled up to PAB's main gate, a Specialist Fourth Class from the newly arrived MP Company stopped the vehicle and asked for identification, strictly in accordance with the standard operating procedures. The officer leaned out of the window and told the MP to get out of the way because he was a commander. The newly arrived MP didn't know the commander from Adam, so he told the officer

[1] In all fairness, I must note that I knew I was not a certified civil engineer when I volunteered to go to Honduras. However, the requirements for the job I filled did not specify special construction or design skills as a prerequisite, only that I be a combat engineer.

that his instructions were to check everyone's ID card, regardless. The combat-arms mentality took over, and the officer got out of the vehicle, calling the kid all kinds of names, threatening his career, and refused to show his ID. The MP stuck to his ground, though, summoning his company commander, who also got an earful of abuse when he arrived to verify personally the colonel's identity. Now, according to the JAG officer, the senior officer was going to follow through with his threats. He had the young guard and the MP commander down in his hootch right then and had ordered the JAG to get down there fast to provide the needed legal veneer. It was some time after the rest of us had gone to bed before the JAG officer came back in. I got up early in the morning before anyone else and left for the States, so I never found out what happened to the dutiful MP.

This particular senior officer represented the upper ranks of the officer corps at PAB. He also labored under the special strains of seniority and command. Most of the officers were quite competent in their fields but were rarely called upon to exercise anything other than moral leadership or, as it is also called, leadership by example. The NCOs were also mainly specialists in their fields. A standard saying, correct in all respects, is that the NCOs are the backbone of the American military, especially its hands-on leadership. But PAB had few lower-ranking enlisted men to be led. Still, it was not hard to pick out those NCOs most likely to be counted on in time of danger.

The new JTFB First Sergeant, a Sergeant First Class (E7), was a heavy-equipment supervisor, an Engineer, who, like the Sergeant First Class in my section, had fulfilled all the requirements for promotion to E8. The new First Sergeant was a rugged, no-nonsense NCO. He tried to run about six miles a day. His mentality was combat oriented, and he had no time for people who were not serious about their military duty. After his first few PT formations, when it became obvious that more than a few officers were excusing themselves and thus setting a bad example, he secured permission for separate formations. If the officers wanted to be flabby and out-of-shape, fine, but he was going to keep the headquarters and headquarters company troops fighting thin. He had a series of run-ins with my Sergeant First Class, who didn't like PT, but the First Sergeant won by a clever combination of force and by utilizing my

86

Sergeant First Class as one senior NCO should use another—as a leader. My NCO was put in charge of accountability for one section at PT.

Main Street, Palmerola Air Base (PAB).

Main Street, F Co., 51st Infantry (Airborne), Bien Hoa, Republic of Vietnam, 1968. (Photo courtesy Gary D. Ford)

Home Sweet Hootch, Building A35.

The common area of A35.

The author's bunk in A35.

The nerve center of PAB—the headquarters offices.

The rusty water tank (on right) built by B company, 39th Engineer Battalion. The smaller tank to the left was PAB's main source of water storage.

The main north-south road in Honduras, snaking through tortuous terrain.

A typical side-hill cut on the main north-south road. Terrain such as this made road-building difficult and dangerous.

Air Guardsman distributing clothing and other items donated by the people of their hometowns.

Tiger Island, in the Gulf of Fonseca.

Honduran family dwelling in the San Lorenzo area.

Starter housing in Tegucigalpa. Rumor had it that American aid paid for at least part of it.

The Navy Seabee dock reconstruction project at Puerto Cortes.

The helipad constructed by the Air National Guard Prime Beef squadron at Cerro La Mole.

B Company, 11th Engineers, improvising scaffolding to construct hangars for the new heliport.

Another fine NCO was a Sergeant First Class in the J2 (intelligence) section. The first time I saw this sergeant, I noticed how quiet and reserved he was. Yet, when he spoke, his voice was full of confidence and his comments insightful. He had a Special Forces patch on his shoulder, but despite his age, no CIB or combat patch. This was unusual, so I asked him about his history.

He had been a combat engineer originally. When he was a staff sergeant, he applied for, and was accepted into Officer Candidate School. He was commissioned into the engineers and sent to the Special Forces qualification course. After being assigned to a Special Forces Group operating in Southeast Asia, he spent several months on a support team for operations in areas outside of Vietnam. Since his actions did not happen in a recognized theater, he did not receive the normal decorations.

After his Southeast Asian tour, he returned to the Engineer Officers Advanced Course. As he was finishing the course and preparing for a new assignment and company command, he was notified that he had been selected for the RIF (reduction-in-force) which followed our withdrawal from Vietnam. He was given two choices—get out of the Army altogether, or revert back to his old NCO rank. Not unlike many of those officers who had been NCOs, he had bought the Army's rhetoric about hard work, personal development, and commitment to a professional career. Given the stark choice, he felt betrayed, wanted nothing more to do with the service, and got out.

About three years later, having become dissatisfied with the pace of civilian life, he reenlisted as a private first class. He had risen back to his current rank fairly rapidly, but it had still taken a decade. He had retained his Reserve commission throughout and was on the verge of being promoted to major on the reserve lists. I told him that, in his second enlistment, I couldn't imagine his platoon leader's reaction upon learning that his newest private was a combat veteran, former NCO, and officer. I also suspect that when he eventually made First Sergeant, his company commander was in for an educational experience, too. This individual was one of several victims of the 1974 RIF that I had met who stayed in or reentered the service as NCOs. In the end, the service meant more to them than their rank.

If NCOs are the backbone of the services, men like the First

Sergeant and the J2 sergeant were the stiffest part. Yet the military has a way of treating such soldiers with less than the respect they deserve. Officers of all ranks were sent to Honduras on a little more than twelve dollars per day in per diem, plus two dollars more per day of separation pay for those with dependents. The twelve dollars was intended to provide some nine dollars for meals, and the remaining three dollars for incidentals. NCOs were sent with only the three dollars (those who qualified got the two dollars separation allowance, too), and were issued a meal card that entitled them to eat free in the mess hall. The rub was that the NCOs lost their separate ration pay, about $155 a month in 1986, in lieu of the meal card. On top of that, almost nobody ate three meals a day in the mess hall. Consequently, TDY in Honduras could be a moneymaking deal for officers who were frugal about where and how much they ate. For NCOs, especially the senior ones with families, Honduran duty often cost them money. Whereas most officers I met had had several weeks to get ready to deploy, many of the NCOs had been given hours, or a few days at the most.

16 March 1986 PAB

One of the young Honduran gate guards shot himself today. Their lack of training is appalling. I was second on the scene. He was shot through the upper thigh. He was more scared than anything else. Wasn't much for me to do except watch. A fireman with a first-aid kit got there seconds after I did. He did a comforting (I'm sure) but poor job of bandaging. It took the ambulance fifteen minutes to get to the site— pisspoor considering it wasn't a half-mile to the hospital. No doctor came. The ambulance had a crew of one, the driver.

The AT '86 and Cabanas folks are becoming more self-sufficient every day. I like watching them work. They have some fine officers and men.

The Honduran military was composed mostly of yearly conscripts who were trained by the units that conscripted them. Consequently, they received very little training before they were issued weapons and told to perform. The U.S. advisors had established a Regional Military Training Center (RMTC) at Trujillo, Honduras, to address just this problem. The center provided consolidated basic training to the conscripts of Honduras and El Salvador to raise the quality of their training. The RMTC also provided some response to the large effort Eastern Bloc forces were putting into the training of the Sandinista Army. The center met with quite some success, but was suddenly closed down at the request of the Honduran government, which became concerned at the number of El Salvadorans, their traditional rivals, being trained on their soil. The U.S. Military Liaison Group (MILGROUP) fervently hoped that the center could be revived.

From what I saw, the Hondurans needed it. On one occasion, my Sergeant First Class and I were traveling around the airfield's perimeter road when we came upon a Honduran security patrol mounted in a jeep. Much to our surprise, the Honduran jeep suddenly pulled over, blocking the road. The Honduran soldiers got out of their jeep, unslinging their rifles. One of them took up a firing position across the hood of the jeep. At this point, the sergeant and I had stopped our truck a few yards away, wondering what rule we had violated. All of a sudden one of the Hondurans fired a round, causing my heart to jump into my mouth. Only then did we realize that his point of aim was oblique to the road, pointing into the ditch. Following the aim, we saw a rabbit running off into the high grass. This occurred at one end of the runway, along the flight path taken by descending aircraft. The rifle was a high-powered, 7.62mm assault weapon. If an American soldier had come back from guard duty without the same number of rounds issued to him, or if that soldier had been so careless as to fire off a round anywhere in the vicinity of an airfield for any reason other than defense of the airfield itself, a swift court-martial would have been the result. As for the young Honduran shot in the guard shack, either he or his partner had been playing with a loaded weapon. These two incidents convinced me that U.S.-provided training was almost a humanitarian cause if it would protect the conscripts from themselves.

Indeed, scuttlebutt had it that the conscripts who guarded the base from lighted guard towers around the perimeter were subject to harsh discipline. If the officer of the guard found them asleep on duty, he had the right to shoot the guard on sight. The first offense, it was said, brought a round to the leg. The second offense required one to the head. These rumors sounded apocryphal, but some Americans at the hospital swore to having treated such wounds. If these accounts contained even a grain of truth, it was criminal to put untrained troops in that position.

7
AHUAS TARA 86

Ahuas Tara '86 was a huge command post exercise (CPX) that raised the number of troops at Palmerola to over thirty-two hundred for a three-week period. The main units that deployed to PAB were elements of the 1st Corps Support Command (COSCOM), the Headquarters Company of the XVIII Airborne Corps, both from Fort Bragg, and the Readiness Command from MacDill Air Force Base, Tampa, Florida. Most of the contingency units of the Army, Navy, Marines, and Air Force with missions in Central America also sent representatives.

The 1st COSCOM was a unit to behold. They deployed with water purifiers; huge, rubber, water-storage blivets; portable showers; and mess halls. In a few short days, the COSCOM elements established a tent city to rival PAB's wooden base camp. The COSCOM actually had better utilities than we did—portable generators supplied all their power needs, and their water storage capacity was twice ours. The other CPX units involved in the exercise depended on the COSCOM for support.

The CPX was one of the main missions for the Lieutenant and me. We coordinated the delivery of all manner of construction supplies for the building of the tent city. We secured from the Hondurans the use of the land. But most importantly, we built latrines. In fact, I became the commander in chief (CINC), latrine, for PAB. I designed my own special, two-hole, forkliftable model, and then contracted to have over seventy-five of the outhouses built. They were the Honduran version of the Porta Potty. I also had dozens of "piss tubes" constructed – a sort of outdoor urinal.

Except for the twenty flush toilets near the task force headquarters, all the other toilets on PAB were burn-out latrines. Human wastes were collected in fifty-five-gallon drums that had been cut in half. The drum halves were filled with diesel fuel before installation in the latrines. Every other day or so, a Honduran work crew belonging to Harbert came along and swapped the barrels. The full ones were taken to several collection points, and the diesel was set afire to burn the wastes. Depending on the weather conditions, a pall of black diesel smoke might overcast PAB for days. On clear, still days, columns of the smoke rose to the sky, marking the burning points.

Piss tubes were six-inch-diameter plastic pipe, planted at an angle into a bed of small gravel. Generally, about six tubes were placed in a row and surrounded by a plywood screen to just above waist level. Pallets provided drip-through flooring. Every so often, the pits were closed and the tubes moved to new locations.

If constructed correctly, the tubes provided a modicum of male privacy and latrine efficiency. However, some of the tubes on base must have been constructed by the smaller Hondurans, who then proceeded not to test them. I first encountered this flawed model on Blackjack, right off the flight line. It was also the latrine closest to the Blackjack mess hall. While waiting for a chopper one morning, I got the urge and hustled to the tubes, undoing my equipment without paying attention to my surroundings. After unlimbering, I noticed that all the tubes were stuck way too far out of the ground. To hit the six-inch opening, I had to back off and fire in a parabola. Worse, after getting started, I noticed that the surrounding screens were as short as the tubes were tall, barely coming up to the level of my waist. There I stood in full view of the open sides of the mess hall, taking target practice. I'm sure a squad of five-foot-tall Hondurans had built the screens, wondering why the crazy Americans were sticking six useless pipes in the ground. They certainly hadn't tried urinating in the tubes, as they would surely have been chest high to the average Honduran.

The doubling of the number of people on the base created special sanitary problems. Naturally, the demand for the unenviable job of shit-burners increased. Additionally, the increased number of latrines meant an increase in the smoke. The hospital's preventive medicine folks had already been on my back about one collection point that lay upwind of a set of hootches. I saw no way out of the problem, as they were the only latrines anywhere close to those hootches. Either the barrels were burned upwind, or the crap had to be hauled all the way through the middle of the small base to the downwind side. The roads through the base being rough, the barrels would slosh their contents along the whole route. The preventive med guys agreed that the burning was the lesser of the two evils.

Since the base was doubling in size temporarily, some of the latrines had to be moved out of one field close to the hospital. This field was being used as the billeting area for most of the seventeen generals coming to the exercise. Moving those latrines brought me my only true notoriety during my assignment.

The latrines and the normal location of their burn point were literally outside the front door of the portable general officers' billets. I had no choice but to move them. So I contracted with Harbert to get the job done. We aimed to move the latrines one hundred meters across the field and downwind of the generals' quarters. However, the latrines being moved were those that the bulk of the female nurses chose to use. Someone had jury-rigged a lighting system in some of the outhouses, despite our consistent remonstrance that only a spark was necessary to light up someone's life. The females liked the latrines because of their proximity and the light—and to hell with the danger. Anyway, the day the forklift showed up to move the latrines, the Lieutenant got a frantic phone call from a female medical service officer. He quickly passed the phone over to me.

"Sir, sir, someone is stealing our latrines!" shouted the female officer. As CINC, latrine, I took this as serious business.

"What do you mean someone is stealing your latrines? Where are you located?" I asked.

"We're across from the Recovery Room Club. A forklift has one of our latrines loaded up right now. But I've got the forklift stopped!" she answered triumphantly.

"Wait a minute! Those are the latrines I just contracted to have moved. They can't stay there. You're just about to be up to your armpits in generals. The preventive med office will never let them stay where they're at. The forklift is just taking them up the field a hundred meters, so let him go."

"But sir, you can't take our latrines!" she shouted.

"Look, Lieutenant," I said in my most authoritative voice, "those latrines are not yours. They're mine. I've got specific orders to move them. Now, you are holding up the execution of a government contract. If you

don't let the forklift proceed, I'll see to it that you pay for the contract."
I do not know if I could have made the charge stick, but the threat worked.

"All right, sir, but you should have asked us first. Could you let us find a place a little bit closer?"

"I don't have to ask you anything, Lieutenant, because you don't own the latrines. But I don't care where the damn things go, as long as they're away from the generals and preventive medicine okays it. Call me right back."

About five minutes later, she called again. "We've got the perfect place. It's about fifty meters down the road towards the airfield, but still convenient to us."

"But the smoke will blow right through the Air Force billets. What does preventive med say?"

"I've got them right here, and they say okay. Also the Air Force detachment commander [also a female officer] likes the new location because it's closer."

This incident could have come right out of "M*A*S*H." It was evidently quite traumatic to the hospital personnel, and had caused quite a stir for a few minutes on that end of base. The hospital commander even authorized a T-shirt to be printed commemorating the day the latrines were saved by the vigilant lieutenant. I was puzzled, though, by the lack of preventive med's concern for the smoke blowing through the USAF billets until I realized that these were also the latrines used by the preventive med detachment. Thereafter, I was duly sensitized to the importance of latrine proximity to a population dense with female servicemembers, especially in an environment where intestinal maladies were common.

23 March 1986 PAB

Cold and blustery the last two days. Had to put tape over the cracks in the hootch walls to keep the dry- season dust from blowing in.

Exercise support is in full swing. The planning for the next two DFTs is about to get hot and heavy- equipment rentals and material acquisitions for Cerro La Mole and Tiger Island.

The vote against the Contra aid bill in the House last week *depressed me. How we can go on spending hundreds of billions of dollars on the defense of Europe, Japan, and Israel, and refuse to spend a miserly $100 million on the defense of our own southern border is beyond me.*

I spent a few hours last night arguing with a lieutenant colonel from the 101st Division general staff down at the AT '86 camp. He sounded like your typically misinformed, vote-grabbing, liberal congressman. He didn't care if Nicaragua was internally communistic or not, as long as they were peaceful. The lieutenant colonel thought the best way to keep them peaceful was through diplomacy. He was afraid of another Vietnam. "I've seen this place before," he said. The lieutenant colonel had no answer for my list of diplomatic overtures made by the United States since 1979, or my list of the lessons of history with respect to dealings with communist nations, except to say that he guessed we couldn't just ignore human rights abuses (especially when I pointed out the righteous breast- beating we indulge ourselves in over human rights in South Africa, the Philippines, et al).

Hootch life continues. The wind blows through too easily. This country experiences amazing cold snaps and wind storms. The life here is not that boring anymore, perhaps because I can see the end. I also occupy my time well. I am getting along well with my hootch mates. As expected in a macho environment, the drinking is heavier than normal; the talk about sex more lurid and more abundant; the tales of prowess more bloated. On a hopeful note, these things are less severe the older one gets.

As PAB's population swelled with the exercises, Hootch A35 gained and lost personnel. The SWO went back to his comfortable, safe weather station in the States. A Philadelphia Irishman replaced him. He was a feisty Celtics fan with thinning red hair, a face almost as red, and a serious demeanor.

Our hootch population also expanded from six to seven. A tall, muscular, African-American, quartermaster lieutenant stayed a couple of days, having to bunk with the TV and refrigerator in our common area. He was then moved over to the logistical support element on Camp Blackjack.

It was at this time that an enigma checked in, and what an enigma. He appeared one day on the spare bunk in the TV area, soused to the gills. He just sat there staring, bobbing and weaving slightly to whatever internal rhythm keeps the inebriated balanced. He had a strange set of eyes that did not help his appearance at all—one eye looked at you and the other one looked for you. The first eye appeared to be functioning and would turn towards whoever was talking. The other eye was milky, and continually strayed, as if searching for an object of focus.

This man's name was Mike, and his first night set the tone for the rest of his short stay. He went to sleep, or passed out early in the evening. Later that night as everyone lay sleeping, Mike got up to go outside. A few seconds later, I heard the unmistakable sound of him urinating right outside the wall by my bunk. As much as the man had drunk, he no doubt was in need. I looked out of the screen, and Mike was hosing down the area under the Infantry Captain's bunk. Mike evidently did not know or remember that he was only fifty yards from the nearest latrine. It was all I could do to keep from laughing because the heat and humidity the next day was no doubt going to give the Infantry Captain's cubicle quite a fragrance—another example of Palmerola justice. I never told the Infantry Captain what happened, but I did share the laugh the next day with the other hootch mates who had suffered from his barbed tongue.

Mike had been a captain for almost 18 years. He worked in Personnel and was sent to PAB from his home base. He seemed a relic, like those ships the Navy keeps mothballed. He was promoted to captain in Thailand during the Vietnam conflict. For whatever reason, he had not been dismissed from the service for failure to progress, but had been given years of continuances until now, when he was close to retirement. Perhaps this was because he had a bronze star. "A Bronze Star!" I asked him incredulously, "Where did you get a Bronze Star?"

"Thailand," he answered, "I was in Thailand, working in personnel. When it got time for me to come home, my boss and I gave each other Bronze Stars."

Mike had a drinking problem. He went through liters of the local Flor de Caña rum every week, augmented every night by beer from the 11th Signal's club, which was two rows of hootches behind ours. His alcoholism colored his every move. In the late afternoons, one could observe Mike as he made his way gingerly down the sidewalk towards the latrine, swaying from one side of the walk to the other, trying to stay on—two steps forward, one to the side, stop, look around, a step back, a step towards the middle, then forward again until he reached the piss tubes. One night right after his arrival, on his first visit to the llth's club, he left with another new arrival to find the latrine. It was dark. Mike was new and didn't know the base at all, and Mike didn't see very well. He and his drinking buddy stumbled around in the dark for a while, then decided to piss behind and on a small building they found. Later that night, Mike, visibly upset, told us what had happened.

"I was standing there pissing, you know . . . ," and his voice would trail off as he lost his train of thought.

"Yeah, Mike, so what happened?" we asked.

"Oh, I was pissing behind this building and someone came up . . ."

"Okay, Mike, so what happened?"

"Well, this guy asked us what the hell we were doing. I said, 'We're pissing! Can't you tell?' ..."

"So what about it, Mike?" someone else said with a little exasperation.

"He wanted to know who we were, so I said, 'I'm a Captain in the Air Force, and who the hell are you?' ..." his voice trailing off yet again.

"Well, goddammit, who was he?!"

"He said he was a Major, the 11th Signal commander, and that we were pissing on his building, his weight room where his troops worked out, and didn't we know that the damn piss tubes were only twenty feet away? Shit, it was so dark I couldn't see anything. He said maybe the colonel would like to hear about insubordinate captains who piss anywhere they want on his compound . . . You don't think the colonel will be mad, do you?"

By this time, the whole hootch was in stitches. This particular Major was quick to anger and zealously protective of his troops and property. From that night on, we gave Mike the nom de guerre of Mad Mike the Pisser, for gallantry in having urinated in close proximity to two of the toughest people on PAB—the Infantry Captain from our hootch and the Major from 11th Signal. Mad Mike worried for days about having to go see the colonel, but nothing came of it.

Mike was actually a super fellow who liked the good life as much as his booze. In the months he was with us, most of his time was not spent working, but on getting himself home early from his tour. He was the organizer of numerous hootch barbecues on a blackened little hibachi someone had left beside the hootch. Often the fare was only hotdogs (dubbed "hootch dogs" or "hootch puppies"), but other times Mike would spring for a few pounds of stringy steak from Comayagua.

One thing, though, you could never do was hold a conversation with him.

"You know guys, this TV show . . . God, I wish I was home . . . You know I was reading the other day. ... I was in Thailand you know. Got a Bronze Star ... I need another beer . . . What do you think about..." was the typical way he began a conversation, and despite any attempt to get him to cohere, he usually didn't, especially if he had been drinking heavily. When he was sent home early, we all missed him. Except for the Infantry Captain.

6 April 1986 PAB

Three months here tomorrow. The border skirmish of two weeks ago illustrates several points.

Most military men want to be involved in a fight, especially those who have never seen war. The fight is what they trained for, been educated for, perhaps even lived for. This is indeed a sad comment on humanity.

Next, you can't fight even a semi-modern war without a proper logistical base. The U.S. troops at PAB were the logistical base this time. We transported the Hondurans; we fueled them; we fed them.

Another lesson is that quick reaction, usually by air insertion, is still the best tactic in low-intensity conflict, especially in guerrilla warfare. This time, the Hondurans were quicker.

Finally, the present, like the past, is seen through many prisms. Almost immediately, the U.S. press began reporting that our government had deliberately blown the incursion out of proportion. Their source was one nameless member of the Honduran government. Likewise, CNN gave prominent coverage to the Nicaraguan denials of crossing the border—bald, bold-faced lies. We at PAB took it seriously.

So did the Honduran military, rightly or wrongly.

My part? I flew out to Jamastran, about seven to ten kilometers from the fighting, to refuel. I was on my way with a few other support personnel to scout some new hilltop locations in case our operations expanded. I was excited, half hoping for accidental action. Stupid? Yes, but nonetheless accurate. I wasn't even armed. We left too quickly, and the arms-drawing procedures take too long. We always stayed one ridge away from the fighting.

One interesting point was the Jamastran airfield. Built for a previous exercise, it could be fixed for use in seven to ten days. Most of our dirt strips are like that. However, using those strips, we could only deploy elements of the 7th Infantry Division (Light), 101st Infantry Division (Air Assault), 9th Infantry Division (Motorized), and the 82d Airborne. Not enough, nor heavy enough to face down all the Sandinos and their allies.

March 1986 was a busy month for the U.S. armed services. In the Gulf of Sidra, the Sixth Fleet challenged Muammar al-Gadaffi's claim to control that significant chunk of the Mediterranean. Almost simultaneously with the start of the Nicaraguan incursion, the Sixth Fleet crossed Gadaffi's "line of death." On March 24 and 25, U.S. naval forces engaged Libyan patrol boats and MiG fighters, and bombed radar installations on the Libyan coast. These actions were part of a deadly dance that continued with Libyan-sponsored terrorist incidents against U.S. citizens in Europe, and culminated with our bombing raid on Gadaffi's capital several weeks later.

On March 22, initial reports filtered in about the Nicaraguan incursion. The Sandinista forces, over two thousand strong, had crossed into Honduras in hot pursuit of a force of Contra rebels. The Hondurans denied that the Contras even existed in their country, so their initial public reaction to the incursion was muted. Since the Contras weren't there, how could they be fighting? Nevertheless, the Hondurans aimed to defend their territory. The new president, Jose Azcona Hoyo, seemed willing to call America's bluff. We had been promising him and his country support. Now he was asking for it. Perhaps upset by Honduras' initial mute response, American officials asked for the request in writing, which they got on 25 March. Specifically, Azcona wanted support to move his troops and artillery to the battlefield. PAB was in good shape to support him because we had all of the extra troops on the ground for AT '86 and Cabanas '86.

The Honduran plan was essentially to isolate the area of the incursion and allow the Sandinos and the Contras to slug it out. Hence, using American airlift, they moved several hundred Honduran infantry and a few pieces of artillery into a cordon around the penetration. The Sandinistas were smart enough not to force the situation. However, unfortunately for the Communists, the Contras slipped a force in behind them, cutting them off from Nicaragua. The battle lasted several days.

Each day at the daily briefing, we got an update from the intelligence people. Far from being the ineffective fighting force portrayed in the media, the Contras were kicking butt. The Sandinistas lost around two hundred casualties in their effort to break out of the encirclement and recross the border. By 27 March, when journalists were finally airlifted to the area, the bulk of the fighting was over, much to their bloodthirsty chagrin.

One day during the incident, I received a call to report to the emergency operation center (EOC), where the American support effort was being run. As I walked into the hootch, I heard the AFFOR talking on the radio. He was confirming the report that had just crackled across the net saying that Soviet-supplied attack helicopters had just lifted off from Sandino Airport in Managua, heading northwest toward the border. I was simultaneously impressed at our intelligence capability and scared that the Communists were about to escalate the incident into a wider conflict by the use of their advanced Soviet weaponry.

The J3 told me to leave immediately for the helipad, where I would meet up with the Grey Wolf commander. He and I were going off to scout the border region near the fighting for possible locations where we could establish support operations if the fighting continued. Great, I thought, here I'm being sent out to scout the border region in an unarmed chopper when the most heavily armed and armored helicopters in the world have lifted off heading in the same direction. Yet, however irrational, I looked forward to the adventure. I remember thinking about a phrase I had read in a World War II B-17 tail gunner's memoirs. He said his mind hated what his guts loved.

The Major in charge of Grey Wolf, myself, and two civilian contract employees working on some of the projects loaded into a UH-60 for the ride. We had to stop to refuel at Jamastran. Upon our approach, I noticed that the force on the airfield was indeed on a war footing. A couple of Army tanker trucks were pulled up under camouflage netting. American GIs in helmets and flak vests, carrying M-16s and M-203 grenade launchers, wandered a perimeter about 100-150 meters from the trucks. The troops were military police from PAB. As the helicopter refueled, I talked to the MP Commander.

I remarked that the airfield was in the middle of a wide-open expanse of ground, with the main danger coming from a tree line about three hundred meters distant. I asked if he had any troops in the trees.

"No, none of mine are over there, but there is a company of Honduran infantry. We're just the interior perimeter. The fighting's only about ten klicks away, you know. What the hell are you doing out here?"

"Yeah, I know where the fighting is. We're doing some recon. The plan is to stay a ridgeline away from the shooting,"

With that said, we were off again.

We flew a pattern through the ridges just north of Jamastran, looking for a field flat enough to land aircraft, but close enough to one of the jagged ridges to provide good overwatch of the surrounding terrain. We checked out a couple of the ridges by dismounting from the helicopter down below, and climbing to the top. The valleys in this area were still quite dry, with little vegetation other than grass. The ridges, on the other hand, were high enough that they were covered with jungle undergrowth and trees of about seventy-five feet in height.

We were a sorry little expeditionary force. I had not drawn a weapon, but the Major and the two civilians were carrying pistols. The helicopter crew also had sidearms, two M-16s and a machete. We were lucky no action came our way. Naturally, when we dismounted from the chopper, we were so green that we forgot the machete. Since I was the biggest, I got to break trail through the dense underbrush. Finally, we found the right field and the right ridge. It was so narrow, though, that the UH-60 could not land. To use the ridge for overwatch meant that Engineers would have to be flown to the top to hack out an area of operations.

The search for Engineers showed how bizarre operating in Central America could get. A small D-4 dozer was available with the CPX contingent from the 101st Division. Our available CH-47 helicopters could lift a dozer that size up to the required altitude. Finding a squad of combat engineers to provide manpower proved to be the real problem. JTFB had a whole battalion of Airborne engineers, the 27th, on the ground at Mocoron in the northeast of the country, building a dirt airstrip as part of the JCS contingency exercise Cabanas '86.

When I asked to borrow a squad, FORSCOM told me that those Engineers had been sent to Honduras only for the exercise they were engaged in and were not available for operations outside the scope of the exercise unless the border situation was declared an emergency. The same was true of the National Guard engineers working on the Yoro road in the north central region of the country. FORSCOM suggested I call Panama to see if SOUTHCOM would allow me to borrow a squad from the 536th Engineer Battalion. The SOUTHCOM Engineer office liked the idea, but the 536th wanted no part of the mission because it was not part of their annual training plan! They refused to help unless ordered to do so. I had always thought that any Engineer unit worth its salt would jump at a chance to do real engineering rather than static training exercises. In the process of arranging the necessary orders, the border incident ended, and with it, the need for expanded operations.

As my diary records, I was not impressed by the media coverage of the border incident. The information put out by the reporters was filled with skepticism at any U.S. or Honduran claims—most of which, the print and broadcast journalists would go to lengths to explain, could not be independently verified. But, as said above, life at PAB had its own little justices. One reporter boarded a C-130, without proper authorization, to fly to Puerto Lempira in Miskitia to cover an influx of refugees prompted by the fighting. I was in the emergency operations center when the pilot radioed in that he had an unauthorized media person on board. Without a second thought, the AFFOR ordered the pilot to deliver him to Puerto Lempira, but not to let him reboard. We chuckled at the man's misfortune. The only way out of that region of Miskitia was by plane or small fishing boat. One could never tell when the next nonmilitary plane might arrive, and the boats were none too seaworthy. That reporter most definitely got a taste of native life before he left. I doubt it improved his reporting.

One very good thing came out of the Sandinista border incursion: Congress voted a new batch of Contra aid, partly in response to Nicaragua's brazen actions.

9 April 1986 PAB

Last week during the big exercise, AT '86, a Lieutenant Colonel from the SOUTHCOM Engineer Office stopped by to talk. He had graduated from high school in 1957 in a class of 190 or so. Sixteen of those will retire, or have retired from the service. The Lieutenant Colonel earned a masters in civil engineering and had worked several years before going to OCS. He said he was in Vietnam in '68, '69, and '70 as an infantry officer. Do we still get such people to enter the service? I wonder.

We talked at length on the strategic situation in CENTAM. The point of AT '86 was to continue demonstrating our resolve to aid fledgling democracies in the region, no matter how politically unsavory this was to some. I compared this fact to the Pacific fleet's actions prior to Pearl Harbor: We can take no defensive actions that might be construed to mean that we seriously contemplate war. To do otherwise is to excite our allies and enemies and antagonize the domestic opposition.

The Lieutenant Colonel perceptively pointed out that at Pearl Harbor none of the aircraft carriers, new cruisers, or subs was in the harbor at the time of the attack. He likened that fact to the current military's pragmatic approach to CENTAM: unofficial defense. He also reminded me that the United States had never had a unanimous declaration of war.

16 April 1986 PAB

Two days after the U.S. attack on Gadaffi. Two quick notes: 1) We should never forget the craven inaction of our "allies," except for steadfast Britain. 2) The prevalent desire in current U.S. society is to avoid personal sacrifice. Yet that avoidance is only made possible by the continued willingness of others to absorb the necessary sacrifices. So it was for Captain Dominicci and Captain Lorence, the crew of the missing FB-111.

America has been defended for most of its history by a small core of professional soldiers and a large host of amateurs called out as the occasions demanded. Only since World War II has the United States needed large numbers of professionals, such as Dominicci or Lorence, to provide most of its security. Yet, in the 1980s, we found that we still needed the amateurs—the National Guard and the Reserves. Most of America's military was oriented on the defense of Western Europe, South Korea, and Japan. Even those forces remaining in the United States spent the bulk of their time practicing to reinforce one of those strategic theaters. Yet, when Latin America came rushing back into our national consciousness, we found ourselves short of resources to make much of an effort. The forces in Panama were already tied to the defense of the Canal. Committing too many Stateside forces to the CENTAM mission might harm the European and Korean reinforcement efforts.

Consequently, most of the American forces operating in Central America in the mid-1980s came from ad hoc arrangements with Stateside units, individual temporary-duty forces such as JTFB, or deployed units of the Guard and Reserve. Many of the stateside units seemed to participate only by being dragged into it, kicking and screaming. They weren't trained for it, nor did it fall within their mission statements.

The individual replacement scheme allowed JTFB to be constructed from scratch without upsetting organizational routines. People were assigned from all over the continental United States and Panama, based on their availability and the task force's needs. It was not unusual to find someone like me there, who had volunteered in order to flee a perceived worse job at his home station. Or, there were others who were simply ordered to Honduras because their unit had been tasked and had sent the best person available. There were also quite a number of those we figured fell into the X man category. That is, a unit gets tasked to send a body, and seizing the opportunity, sends its deadweight, its riffraff, its least useful, thus ridding itself of a potential problem for several months.

The Guard and the Reserve, though, seemed to jump at real missions. Several key members of the task force staff were individual ready reservists (IRR) who had volunteered for six-month tours. The head chaplain, an IRR member, had been there for more than a year. Two other staffers, one a Sergeant and the other a Major, were retired policemen. Reserve medical detachments or individuals made common appearances for two weeks at a time throughout the year.

The true workhorses, though, were the Guard Engineers working on the Yoro road project. This project was a multiyear, joint Honduran-American effort to bring an isolated valley into contact with the central commercial corridor of the country. Named Blazing Trails, in 1986 the Missouri National Guard provided a new battalion of Engineers every two weeks for about five months and did an outstanding job. Moreover, reservists supervised the loading and shipping of the Guard equipment both to and from the States. Other Guard and Reserve units from Arkansas and Oregon also came to conduct joint exercises with the Hondurans.

Several of the U.S. governors, most notably in Maine and Massachusetts, refused to allow their Guardsmen to train in Honduras. These governors eventually brought suit in federal court to stop the deployment of their units to Honduras, essentially because they disagreed with the Reagan administration's policy toward Nicaragua. I guess it horrified them to think that their state troops were actually being used as a show of force against a country whose capital city had been declared the sister of many cities in their own states. Most importantly, though, when America was in need, her citizen soldiers once again answered the call.

18 April 1986 PAB National Prayer Breakfast Day

This morning I went to the National Prayer Breakfast in the mess hall. Pretty standard fare: an invocation, a few hymns in English and Spanish, an address by a guest speaker, and remarks by the commander.

The guest speaker was one I'll remember for a long time. He was Bishop Leopold Frade, Anglican bishop of Tegucigalpa. The bishop was an American, but Cuban by birth. He left Cuba as a teenager to escape church persecution. He had brought with him eight young Nicaraguan draft dodgers.

Bishop Frade's message was that these young boys, the oldest being no more than seventeen, had stories that needed telling. The bishop estimated that Honduras was the sanctuary for about 133,000 Nicaraguan refugees, thousands of them draft dodgers or deserters. He implored us to take the stories home with us, just as visiting newspapermen should. But he knew too well where to find most reporters—in Tegucigalpa's bars, which led him to question if they were sober when they write what they do about the Nicaraguan conflict.

The boys were a patriotic lot, a quality not uncommon among political exiles. The oldest boy described how the draft worked: any male sixteen to forty was obliged to serve in the regular forces. However, recently, he said, the selection depended more on physical size than age. Everyone else is forced to serve in the militia. One of the youngest, only fourteen, described being impressed while at school. His family did not hear of his whereabouts for a month and a half.

Someone asked what the boys thought of the Contras. Basically, they felt that the Contras were doing good. Furthermore, the Contras were taking care of many of the refugees. Given arms, the Contras would be able to hit the Sandinistas harder.

Another question was asked about their families. The oldest boy, the unappointed spokesman, told of reprisals against the families of deserters. The reprisals generally take the form of increased surveillance by the state security police and the local Committee for the Defense of the Revolution, a perverse parody of a neighborhood block organization. Also, their families suffered reductions in ration allocations.

The JTFB commander rose to conclude in his own fashion. He pointed out that the Contras were a voluntary organization whereas the Sandinista army existed through forced conscription. The commander also contended there was no draft in El Salvador, only a minimum one in Honduras, and none in the United States. (The El Salvadorans do have a draft, and we have Selective Service registration.) The Chaplain had the final word before the benediction; he said that the American most admired by the boys was Madonna.

Female soldiers were an integral part of Palmerola's operations. Every section on base from the armed MPs to the MI battalion had some. They functioned as clerks, chaplain assistants, nurses, supply officers, pilots, and in at least two instances, commanders.

One scholarly observer[25] who had visited PAB prior to my arrival wrote, "Women worked as effectively as men . . . Some of the female soldiers worked less effectively than most soldiers, but then so did some of the men." Further observations included that as more time was spent at PAB, the women were increasingly accepted as individuals and decreasingly seen as members of their own sex. Also, the one persistent problem area was physical fitness training, particularly running.

When women were put in the rear of a running formation, too many fell out. When females were put in the front, the males perceived that they were being held back.

At this point in the 1980s, females were denied the privilege of serving in purely combat-oriented specialties such as fighter pilots, sailors on surface combatants or in submarines, infantry, cannon crewmen, or combat engineers. Like so much else in the service, these distinctions verged on the fictitious. Women were not allowed to get killed in a fighter, but they could get shot down in a transport plane. They could not fire cannon, but they could deliver the ammunition to the cannon. Just because a woman could not be an infantryman does not mean that an infantry brigade headquarters, only a few kilometers from the front, wouldn't have several assigned to it. Since PAB was dominated by the support branches of the services, the proportion of women was quite evident.

Yet, perhaps this seemingly arbitrary distinction has some validity to it. In my observations, the women servicemen in Honduras functioned well for the most part. However, their jobs were generally technical, not physical, nor did their jobs require much in the way of assertive leadership. For some reason in the mid-80s, male and female servicemen were held to different physical standards, at least in the Army. A woman between the ages of twenty-seven and thirty-one had to do less than half as many push-ups as a man to stay in the service, even though the two might be assigned to perform the exact same job.

Other disparities were allowed for running and sit-ups. Pregnancy was its own special problem in the service. Men naturally viewed the lower physical standards and the allowances made for pregnancy as the women "getting over," especially if a male lost a job to a woman he knew was less physically capable.

Then there was psychology. To the average American, it came as no surprise that men and women do not form the same kinds of bonds between the sexes as they do among people of their own gender. Maybe that is why in an age when the emphasis had been on making public and private institutions integrated and coed, some colleges were still allowed to be totally female, but all-male social clubs were considered discriminatory. Perhaps that is why we still had a male infantry.

Sometimes the differences between men and women in the services were brought into sharp relief at Palmerola. The battle over the latrines was one such case. Another case also concerned the medical detachment, the Engineers, and one of the highest-ranking female officers on base.

One day in late April, I had been driving around the base when I noticed what appeared to be a new, but crudely built hootch in the hospital area. I drove over behind the building, which was attached to one of the hospital's regular buildings. Whoever had slapped the thing up had been trying to follow the general design of most of the wooden buildings on Palmerola, but none too successfully. The add-on had a slight lean to it; its only foundation was a few 2"-by-4" stilts resting on narrow blocks of wood. The building was a disaster waiting to happen. The first time a stiff wind blew, or the medical staff put any kind of load onto the floor, the building was going to collapse. I hustled back to the office to make sure that no one had authorized a self-help building, or that this was not a contract job done horribly. It was neither. Evidently, the hospital had got the lumber from somewhere and had done a little slipshod construction on its own. This brought up the interesting question of where they got the lumber, since the Engineer section controlled the only Class IV (construction materials) yards on base.

We immediately called up the hospital operations staff to find out what was going on. Yes, they were adding onto one of their storage buildings. We asked who had authorized the construction, and their reply was that their commander had. Of course, commanders were not supposed to do that because the buildings they commissioned were generally built to the same quality of the new one at the hospital—death traps on shaky foundations with shoddy, backyard wiring. We let the operations officer know that the JTFB commander's standing order on base was that no buildings were to be put up without the Engineer office's approval and quality control. Our next question concerned the construction supplies and their origin. We had a couple of deployments coming in the middle of May, which were going to build several new wooden buildings, and the lumber had been ordered for that purpose. Additionally, our lumber budget for the year had recently been cut back. Well, the operations officer could confidently reply that they had got the lumber in an authorized manner—from an engineering NCO! Our orders to the hospital were to take the building down and return the lumber.

This newest battle between the hospital and the Engineers raged for most of the day at the higher levels of command. Did we really need the lumber? Can't the hospital please convert some of their canvas storage areas to wood? Now that they had the building up, couldn't they just fix the deficiencies? No, the building would have to be built over from scratch. The art of compromise continued until the commander authorized the hospital to rebuild the building under the quality control of the Engineers. Great, we thought, everyone on post was going to start carting off our lumber ... At least the NCO in charge and I had a heart-to-heart talk about his lumber- yard.

A day or so after the battle of the building, the office was hot and quiet. I was working on the paperwork for the coming deployments. One of the clerks was typing documents, when a short, female lieutenant colonel and a tall, male second lieutenant walked through the hootch door. She had fire in her eyes and a certain set to her jaw that suggested that I should "pop to" (the position of attention) and report.

"Good afternoon, ma'am, I'm Captain Waddell. How can I help you?"

"Captain Waddell, I'm the head nurse here at Palmerola," she began slowly, picking up speed as she went. "I just wanted to stop by and tell you that I'm tired of your office contravening everything that we try to do to better the lifestyle of the hospital personnel or our patients. It's like you and your office have it out for us."

She paused, almost breathless, as if waiting for me to reply.

"Ma'am, I'm not sure what you mean," I replied meekly, but I suspected that I did know.

"You Engineers refuse to help us! Every time we ask you to do some simple repair, fix some of our buildings, or do anything for us, you find some way not to. Then, when we try to help ourselves, you thwart us, just like you did with the new storage building." She was on the verge of shouting now, but I didn't really care. I had eaten enough dirt over the previous four months for trying to do my job safely and legally.

"Ma'am," I began, trying to keep my voice steady, "we keep a record here of every work order that is requested of us. The hospital is one of the biggest units on base, so you can imagine how many orders you all generate. If you would like, I'll show you the book and how many work orders have been accomplished at the hospital, and for what cost. I think you'll be surprised at just how much we've done for you. As for thwarting your efforts at self-help, ma'am, engineering is a profession, just like nursing. We have our own professional standards and codes for construction. That's why when I see a building like the one you people put up the other day, I get concerned. The damn thing was going to collapse on you. Your people also have a tendency to rewire everything they own. The result has been two fires, one at the hospital, and one in the nurses' hootches."

"Well, we need lights along our walkways so we can wheel our patients at night. It's safety. If you would just give us the lights, we wouldn't have the problems. We arranged to have the lights put in, but you made us take them out."

Her voice was choking now.

"That's my point, ma'am. You just can't wire up additional light circuits indefinitely. Eventually you run out of electricity, get an overloaded circuit, and then a fire. The hospital's problem is lack of power distribution. Yet one of your people got the Readiness Command contingent in the last exercise to wire up a lighting system for your walkway. When the circuit burned, you had somebody else rewire the circuit box in the same way. That's why we told you to take it down. You were lucky you didn't burn down half of the base. Look, ma'am, we don't come over and pass judgment on how you treat your patients, nor do we offer our medical advice, which you don't need. Leave the engineering to us."

I had tried to keep my voice as steady and professional as possible, but whenever you are dealing with higher-ranking officers, they have all the advantages. I thought her ass-chewing was going to continue, but, all of a sudden, her eyes clouded up, she began to cry, and she ran from the hootch. Throughout this exchange, the second lieutenant she had in her tow had been punctuating her remarks with emphatic nods. I didn't like the looks of the guy. He looked after the running nurse with much astonishment. Then, he turned to face me.

"Well, sir, I specifically asked to have my pharmacy air-conditioned back in March, and nothing has happened so far. Do you know how expensive and important my pharmaceuticals are? Now when is the air- conditioning going to be put in?" Jesus Christ, I thought, save me from these hospital people.

"Look, Lieutenant," I said, none too kindly—I had the advantage of rank now. "Like I just told the head nurse, you have a goddamn power problem. Your circuits are already overloaded. And as even you can understand, air-conditioning requires some sort of electricity. You'll have to wait for the hospital to be rewired, which is supposed to happen later this year. Some of it will be done next month by an Air National Guard unit, but not enough."

"But, sir," he whined, "I've talked to Panama, and they said to tell you that I had to have my pharmacy air- conditioned."

"Hey, great! Since you have all that pull with Panama, just call them back and tell them to send me enough money and exterior electricians for the project, and we'll have it done lickety-split. Myself, I haven't had any luck with 'em at all."

About this time, the head nurse walked back in, drying her eyes.

"I'm sorry, I don't usually get this emotional, but I wanted your office to know how we felt about the level of support we have been getting. Good day."

She and her escort left the hootch. My poor clerk finally closed his mouth, which had been hanging open for the previous ten minutes. Was she indicative of the quality of females in the service at Palmerola? I don't think so, but she had a reputation for being one of the best and had made lieutenant colonel fairly quickly, judging by her age. Maybe she'd just had a bad day.

27 April 1986 PAB

Back from Tampa two days ago. Ate all kinds of good food. The conference at Readiness Command was a different matter. Nine units or higher headquarters were involved. Nine lieutenant colonels, five majors, and four or five captains came. The whole purpose of the conference was to develop a memorandum of understanding (MOU) on the deployment and use of a thirty- to-thirty-five-man Engineer platoon at PAB. Talk about overkill! Bureaucracy wins another!!!

I saw another thing worthy of comment. On a national newsbreak on one of the networks, the major topics that stood out were a Joan Baez protest concert in Houston that drew forty or fifty people, and a mindless tidbit about Michael Jackson's personal life. What makes these items so interesting is that Baez drawing forty or fifty people to an anti-Contra protest gets national news time. How can anyone say there is no news bias if some rather insignificant pro-Contra gathering doesn't get the exact same amount of coverage, which it rarely, if ever, does. Did Bishop Frade's visit to us get any notice? Of course not. As for Michael Jackson, this example is, in essence, one of our problems. We ignore the serious in favor of the frivolous.

The conference included officers from Readiness Command (REDCOM), Forces Command (FORSCOM), Southern Command (SOUTHCOM), the 36th Engineer Group from Fort Benning, Georgia, the 937th Engineer Group from Fort Riley, Kansas, the 20th Engineer Brigade from Fort Bragg, North Carolina, the 11th Engineer Battalion at Fort Belvoir, Virginia, the 193d Infantry Brigade from Panama, and two of us from JTFB. If an elephant is only a horse designed by a committee, then we were lucky that we didn't produce a helluva pachyderm. In reality, the decision to station an Engineer platoon at PAB was the crowning achievement of the Engineer office during my tour.

PAB was maintained on a daily basis by the forces of Harbert International according to a services contract. Yet no contract can cover all contingencies. Hence, when something broke, or something needed constructing that fell outside the contract, an expensive modification of the existing contract had to be negotiated, or a new contract sent to at least three firms for bidding—or, if the estimate was less than a thousand dollars, we could sole-source the work to Harbert, but their charge was always near the full thousand. None of these options conformed to the usual military need for expeditious problem solving. To make matters worse, several pieces of Army engineer equipment had been left at PAB: a forklift and a road grader being the most valuable. Some wise guy, though, had assigned this equipment to Harbert as part of the contract!

So, if PAB needed a piece of this Army equipment for some reason, no matter how minor, we had to rent it back from Harbert. I always wanted to find the idiot who had drawn up that contract.

Often the answer demanded of us by the units working on PAB was to do the work inside our own office. After all, we were Engineers weren't we? Unfortunately, we had none of the men, equipment, or time to do most of the jobs. Hence, one of our consistent complaints to SOUTHCOM was the lack of Engineers at PAB just to do work as it came up. As with my conversations over the deployment of the 245th Utilities Detachment, the answer kept coming back that units could only be sent to PAB to perform scheduled, resourced, well-planned training that had been identified for months. However, the two lieutenant colonels that we dealt most with from the 193d and SOUTHCOM, both in Panama, well understood our predicament, having made numerous trips to PAB themselves. Slowly, a plan evolved that would meet Army regulatory and fiscal requirements, but would also provide an operational capability to the base. That was the reason for the conference at MacDill AFB in Tampa.

All of the units and organizations at the conference had a stake in the decision. This should give one an idea of the complexity of the daily activities at PAB. Everyone had some small slice of the pie, and this was just the Army side of it. SOUTHCOM controlled all U.S. military activities in Central and South America, with the 193d Infantry Brigade, the Army component of SOUTHCOM, controlling all Army activities. FORSCOM controlled all Army activities in the Continental United States (CONUS). I never figured out exactly where REDCOM fit in the bureaucratic layering. The two Engineer Groups were essential to our plans. The 20th Engineer Brigade was the unit responsible for contingency planning and operations in Central America, just in case we went to war. The 11th Engineers were going to be the first unit providing a platoon to PAB. As for JTFB, all we wanted was an Engineer platoon and some equipment.

I have mentioned elsewhere the problems caused in the Engineer office by the rapid personnel turnover and the constant undermanning. The office had no institutional memory. New officers and NCOs spent the first thirty days of their tours saying, "I'm sorry, but my predecessor must have promised you that, or ordered this, or contracted for that, but I don't have the foggiest idea what you're talking about." Worse, expensive, time-consuming designs and surveys got lost or misplaced in the shuffle. All the work was being done piecemeal. The plan, as it worked out, was to put the two engineer groups in charge of all engineer support in Central America on a six-month rotating basis. This way, a higher engineer headquarters would be responsible for supporting us with designs and survey teams, record keeping of the completed work, and would provide oversight to the platoon assigned to PAB. The platoon would be provided on a sixty-day rotating basis from one of the battalions under control of the Engineer Groups. Their complement of equipment would stay in place as the personnel changed and equipment would be swapped out every six months with the change of control.

That was the healthy result of the conference. My diary entry at the time had been too pessimistic. Of course, the units involved had to make sure that their troops would be fed, housed, and not worked to death, that their equipment would not be lost, and that the deployment would not screw up some really important European-oriented exercise stateside. The 20th wanted to make sure that the deployed platoon did not do any of the missions assigned to units in contingency exercises.

To get around the fiction of operations versus training, our office had come up with some huge projects, expected to occupy the platoons through several deployments. One was to construct a chain link fence around the whole of PAB. Another was to reconstruct PAB's perimeter road. Plans also included conversion of some of the tent billets into wooden structures. Any manpower or equipment not involved in these training events—and we made sure such assets would be available—could then be employed in "opportunity training," or what one could have called "operations." This could mean filling in the gaps of the Harbert contract, working on the TACAN road, etc. It was almost insulting to our integrity to be forced into this linguistic manipulation by overly officious bureaucratic rules. One could say the whole conference was due to this distinction between the words "operations" and "training."

In this same period of time, when the base facilities were under increased strain due to the exercise and DFT load, our power problems continued. The FESA detachment, back for another deployment, was working furiously to construct a new power station that would supply PAB's power needs in an emergency. The plant consisted of two 750-kilowatt generators, each the size of a small building. The plant's completion, though, was still several weeks away. In the meantime, the power outages continued to annoy us and exacerbate our water problems. In fact, the power surges accompanying the return of power began to burn out our water pumps.

I have already mentioned that when the power went off, water was rationed until the tanks refilled. If the pumps burned out, rationing continued until we replaced the pumps. This was no easy job. The pumps were sunk in several wells around PAB. Harbert could pull the pumps out of the ground, but the Engineer office had to acquire new ones. The only place pumps were available was in San Pedro Sula. Hence, when a pump went out, an Engineer vehicle hit the road for the six-hour round trip.

I made several such trips with an Air Force Staff Sergeant. He had rotated in for a ninety-day tour. He was extremely conscientious and he had excellent judgment. Unlike so many of us, his attitude was always positive. He was the kind of soldier that most commanders dream of. He became an expert at dealing with the hardware shop where we got the pumps.

Many of the merchants in San Pedro were of Arabic descent. It was said that they fled Palestine after each of the two world wars, when Arab-Israeli problems flared up. Many of them were apparently Christians. Since our dealings were fairly technical, the language barriers were comical. Eventually, the shop owner gave the NCO and me a Spanish dictionary. This did little good, though, because it was entirely in Spanish.

The pump problem was yet another illustration of the problems that U.S. forces had in supporting themselves in an ad-hoc manner in Central America. These problems were largely the result of a lack of long-term planning. We were paying about three thousand dollars for each pump we bought. The pumps had been made in Seneca Falls, New York, and sold stateside for about eight hundred dollars. Yet we did not have, nor could we get, authorization to buy the pumps from the factory, have them shipped to the nearest air base with regular flights to Central America, and delivered to PAB. We figured that the factory cost and the shipping would be far less than what we were paying. As mentioned above, even when the pumps were operational, we had less water production and storage capabilities than the COSCOM unit that deployed during Ahuas Tara '86. Yet the COSCOM capability was short term, and we needed a long-term solution. We hoped that the power station would be the fix.

27 April 1986 PAB (Continued)

A thought on the recent prayer breakfast: the activity of the churches against communism in Central America does not receive nearly as much publicity as the activity of U.S. churches against further U.S. involvement in Central America. Now, saying that protesting U.S. activities that are designed to combat communism is wrong is not to imply that the protesters are procommunist. However, what the protestors are doing, should they be successful, will be of great aid to the communists.

From a poll published in a recent newspaper: a majority of those polled opposed aid to the Contras. The real significance, though, was that only 25 percent knew whose side we were on. How could the people polled make a good decision if only one-fourth knew who we were aiding? How many of the 25 percent supported aid? The poll didn't say.

I am amazed now at the bitterness I expressed in my diary about church activities or about the anti-involvement protests. Yet American involvement in Central America was the key emotional issue of most of the 1980s. The views on both sides tended towards the extremes. Many will dismiss the view above as just another opinion from a neo-McCarthyite, which it obviously is not. I am no more a McCarthy disciple than most of the protesters were procommunist. However, whatever the intent of those protesting our involvement, the effect was to make the work of the military more difficult, and to produce the kinds of doublespeak someone in power saw as necessary, for example, in the arbitrary distinctions between operations and training. It is interesting to note that during the Vietnam War, General Westmoreland voiced what was surely a common feeling among military personnel in April 1967. Speaking at a dinner hosted by the Associated Press, the general said that "Through a clever combination of psychological and political warfare," the enemy had gained worldwide public support "which gives him hope that he can win politically that which he cannot accomplish militarily."[26] He further asserted that flag burners and other antiwar protesters were encouraging the enemy, and thus raising the costs of war for America, especially in terms of American lives. Westmoreland was vilified for such statements. But the sentiment was similar to many expressed by military personnel about our efforts in Honduras. Thankfully, we were not engaged in a shooting war in Central America. But you don't have to be a rocket scientist to figure out that the Sandinistas and FMLN took more than a little comfort from the domestic American political turmoil over our Central American policies.

On the other hand, it may be fairly argued that whatever the intentions of those of us who served in uniform, our effect was to enable the corrupt elites of Central America to continue their control over their societies. My only answer to that was that the policies adopted in this period by our elected government, however acrimonious the debates among the branches, reflected a favoring of evolution over revolution—the former being far less bloody in the short and the long runs. Indeed, from my perspective, the principal error of most of the protesters was in mistaking Marxist-Leninist-inspired revolution as some more benign form of "socialist development"—certainly an oxymoronic construction. In the churches involved in the protests, the error was in mistaking the Sandinista revolution as one that was "doing God's work," which is the mistaking of a temporal regime for one that is spiritual. It seems incredible that liberation theology, the ideas of which provided the underpinnings for much of the religious protests, could link Marxian class analysis with theology and not be seen— based on the empirical evidence of places such as Eastern Europe, the Soviet Union, and Cuba—as a compact with evil itself.[27]

As for the fact that some churches and religious organizations opposed the Sandinistas and FMLN, most of the attention went, rightly so, to Cardinal Miguel Obando y Bravo of Managua, who consistently opposed what the Ortega brothers proposed for his country. And he was not alone. Yet many of those who supported U.S. policy, or at least opposed the Marxists, were too often dismissed as just fundamentalist kooks (fundamentalist Christians, conservative Catholics, and Mormons seem to be the only groups in the United States still considered to be fair game for open criticism and satire by mainstream media and politicians) or visceral anticommunists not possessed of good reason— throwbacks to an earlier, unenlightened era of the Cold War. As Bishop Frade eloquently demonstrated, though, high-minded opponents of communism did exist.

During the dry season, the scourge of PAB was dust. It got into everything. In places, the fine powder was easily six inches deep. PAB dry seasons also brought wind storms that produced a haze of dust that hung in the air for days. It had particularly deleterious effects on sensitive items like aircraft engines. The fixed-wing aircraft stationed at PAB were lucky in that they had the use of existing and temporary hangars; the helicopters had one small, dilapidated maintenance tent. When the wet season arrived, the dust turned into mud. The bottom literally fell out of portions of the perimeter road. Consequently, regardless of the time of year, the pilots, crew, and maintenance sections assigned to the helicopters suffered the elements.

In May, B Company of the 11th Engineers deployed to PAB to construct a heliport. This unit was also to provide the first rotational engineer platoon. Their advanced party arrived early and constructed several hootches as permanent Engineer billets. Survey teams went to work immediately on the chain-link-fence project.

When the main body of the company arrived, work began in earnest on the heliport. The project involved leveling a piece of ground along the main runway. Then, over a thousand sheets of M8A1 steel matting had to be laid to create the helipad. Each sheet weighed around 110 pounds, and manual labor was the only method. Next, two portable hangars had been purchased in Canada and flown to PAB for assembly. Each was a steel skeleton with a huge sheet of synthetic fabric stretched over the girders and tied down to anchors. The M8A1 matting was from the Vietnam era. Only a few of the older NCOs in the company had ever seen it used. The hangers were also new to the company. Nevertheless, the company had done research and training in the limited time it had before deployment. Additionally, the company commander was a licensed professional engineer. Because of their preparations, the heliport was completed with few glitches, a truly professional job. Everyone from the executive officer of the 11th, a Major, on down humped matting in the tropical heat.

The month of May, like March, was a busy month at PAB. In June the rains began, so there was a rush to complete the remaining projects and exercises. The huge road project in the Yoro valley wound down as the Reserve and Guard units involved added finishing touches to the year's work and began the arduous process of out-loading their equipment through the mountains to Puerto Cortes.

The 2nd Battalion of the 75th Rangers from Fort Lewis parachuted onto the new dirt strip that had been constructed in Mocoron by the 27th Engineers. This was the second phase of Cabanas '86. The purpose of the assault jump was to practice what the Rangers had done at Grenada (and what U.S. soldiers did again during Operation JUST CAUSE in Panama, December 1989). The Rangers then conducted jungle training and joint patrolling with the local Honduran battalion. The Rangers brought an engineer platoon from the 27th back with them to repair the strip, which had been washed out in places during the early rains. This platoon lost one of its D-5 dozers when the chutes broke off the equipment at about a thousand feet. The dozer ended up buried in the mud.

May also brought the only two casualties of the U.S. effort in the first six months of 1986. The first was a Special Forces NCO who was training a Honduran unit on escape and evasion. Apparently, the NCO and another American soldier "captured" one of the Hondurans. In the ensuing scuffle, the Honduran killed the first NCO and seriously wounded the second with a knife. The second death was far more mysterious. A young Ranger Spec Four climbed into his pup tent with his Ranger buddy one night near Mocoron, and the next morning he was dead. There were no apparent wounds or other causes.

Many of the jobs at PAB, or in Honduras, were hazardous, but nobody actually expected to die. Such events had a sobering effect on morale generally, and weighed heavily on the leadership specifically. Both deaths occurred within a few days. I remember passing the Air Force Forces Commander (AFFOR) on a sidewalk at this time. I tossed off a typical "How's it going, sir?" He did not respond with the usual "Just fine . . ." or "Great!" On this occasion, he responded, almost muttering, "It'll be a lot better when our people stop getting themselves killed ..."

My Sergeant First Class and I made an inspection trip to Puerto Cortes in the midst of all of this activity.

We went for several reasons. The equipment for B Company, 11th Engineers, was arriving on one of the ships that was also being used to take home a load of equipment from the completed Yoro road project. Additionally, a naval mobile construction detachment (the Seabees) was recuperating a section of the Puerto Cortes pier. Finally, we just needed to get out of PAB for a couple of days.

Puerto Cortes was a filthy, smelly little backwater on the Caribbean coast. It served as a principal port for the Honduran Navy. It was also a key shipping point for much of the fruit that left Honduras. Hence, it was a terminus for one of the small railway lines running along the north shore. From the air, it was not unusual to see several miles of boxcars, with DOLE stamped on them, lined up on the rails waiting to be loaded onto ships. The little port could also unload fuel tankers and large cargo ships. These facilities made the port of prime importance to the U.S. effort.

There was not much else to recommend the place. It did have free-port status, but that seemed to consist of a couple of factories operating behind chain link fences near the piers. Some of the locals said that the factories made baseballs for the American market. A couple of streets near the piers on the eastern side of the port served to lubricate and entertain the crews that stopped there.

Upon our arrival, the sergeant and I went to find a place to eat lunch. Being tired of the standard fare of frijoles, tortillas, pollo (chicken), and bife (beef), we had hoped to find a decent seafood eatery. We ended up at a place on the shore, an older building that had recently been re-modeled. We were the only customers in the place. We sat at a line of tables, each with a thatched canopy, along the sandy beach. The meal was entirely forgettable, but the beer was cheap and the scenery beautiful. It was a tableau out of a depressing, cheap novel—two soldiers alone in a strange land, drinking, being waited on by Latin waiters, watching the sunset over a watery horizon.

Most of the American soldiers and sailors manning the port unloading-and-outloading effort were from the Reserves. Even though they were part-timers, they knew their business well. The equipment was marshaled in orderly fashion, prepared for loading, then loaded; likewise, in reverse. Exactly as in the case with Engineer units, the Army found it hard to support itself logistically outside of CONUS, Europe, or Korea without heavy usage of the Reserves.

The officer in charge of the advance party from the 11th Engineers had gone through the Engineer Officer Basic Course with me. He was still a second lieutenant and had some good NCOs with him. I found them bunked down in a warehouse near the ship. The next day, he and his crew were going to ferry the bulldozers, earthmovers, and trucks for the heliport project to PAB. To do this, they had to take the only improved north-south road available—it only had two lanes. In some places it didn't have shoulders, and it snaked over several mountain ridges. All of the heavy equipment was being moved on forty-ton lowboy trailers towed by M-916 or M-920 semi tractors. To add to the fun, the loads were outsized. The crews' only experience with driving in Honduras had been on the three-hour trip north from PAB. I told my classmate to place clearly marked vehicles ahead of and behind the convoy, and by all means stick to slow speeds. As this is standard Army procedure, he must have thought I was loony to make the long trip to the port just to tell him that. But driving in the States or in Europe was nothing like driving on the chaotic roads of Central America. I thought it worth emphasizing anyway. The convoy did make it to PAB safely, but at the cost of quite a few tires and frayed nerves.

The Seabees were rebuilding a section of the Honduran Navy pier. The sailors were pounding in new piles to anchor the pier and running a new concrete cap on the docks. They had set up their tents in a lot nearby. An American Chief Petty Officer was actually assigned to advise the Honduran units in the area. He was quite astute, and I was surprised to find that he did not hold a higher rank. For protection, he carried a tiny revolver on his hip. He functioned as the liaison between the Seabee detachment commander and the local Hondurans. There were several such Americans serving on these types of assignments in the country.

The Seabees had been sent down under separate instructions from those of the Army Engineers. Yet JTFB was supposed to exercise some control over them—hence the purpose of our visit. In reality, there was very little that we could do to affect their work. They were entirely self-sufficient, and their liaison had them well provided for.

After checking on these happenings, the sergeant and I went to check into the local hotel. It had seen better years, but was still luxurious by Honduran standards. We made contact there with yet another American soldier outposted to the area, a Sergeant (E-5). He actually was assigned to the J4 (logistics) section at PAB. Since there was so much activity going on at the port, he had been sent to Puerto Cortes on extended TDY to act as a liaison. He was of Panamanian heritage and spoke Spanish fluently. Again, here was an example of a very junior soldier entrusted with enormous responsibility. He reported nothing unusual to us about the cargo operation then underway.

Because he was fluent in Spanish and was obviously Hispanic himself, the locals readily accepted him. He suggested that we go out and see the town—what there was of it. We traveled a couple of blocks over to where the ship was docked. Across the street was a string of bars, handy for crews with a limited amount of liberty time. We went into one building that opened onto an inner courtyard filled with small tables. We ordered beers and were immediately besieged by short, ugly women - the bar's prostitutes. The logistics Sergeant said that for a few dollars, one could rent both a girl and a room on the second floor of the courtyard. Even though my Sergeant First Class was having fun teasing one young lady, I suggested we drink up and find a better location.

The logistics Sergeant directed us to a street a couple of blocks inland from the docks. This bar was clean. The customers were dressed much better than we were, and modern American music was blasting through a stereo system. The drinks were much more expensive, and according to our local guide, so were the girls. Just as in the dive, young women immediately descended on us, asking us to buy them drinks, rubbing up against us, sitting on our laps. The logistics Sergeant informed us that, being a small, well-used international port, there wasn't a place in the town that didn't offer the same amenities. Only the prices and decor differed. I'm quite sure that I dampened the fun that the two sergeants, both single, might have had. We ended up drinking beer at a booth built along the street. It was a continuation of the same bad novel we began earlier in the day, but without the scenery—soldiers go to run-down bars, continue drinking, get accosted by women of the night. The next morning, we left to return to PAB.

The inaugural deployment of the Air National Guard Prime Beef engineers also occurred in May. Their deployment continued the fine seat-of-the-pants engineering being done in Central America, but also caused the next humorous controversy—the bathtub incident.

When SOUTHCOM proposed the use of the Air Guard, we had several projects that desperately needed work: Cerro La Mole needed repairs; the PAB hospital needed a complete rewiring of its power distribution system; several headquarters huts needed extensions; and the females needed their own showers. Perhaps most important, the flight line lacked sufficient grounding rods for truly safe operation. The JTFB Engineering office assigned all of these projects to the Air Guard unit assigned to the first deployment.

This particular Air Guard unit was a base civil engineering squadron that was normally split between the Capitol City Airport in Springfield, Illinois, and Chicago O'Hare. When deployed, these squadrons are called "Prime Beef." Regular soldiers are generally condescending to part-timers, refusing to believe that anyone working only 39 days a year can do as well as a full-time soldier who works 365 days. Yet the technical competency of this squadron was superb. Many of their members held civilian jobs comparable to their military duties, as is often the case with technical units in the Reserve Components. Hence, the unit had fuel technicians and pavement specialists, for example, who did such work full-time as civilians. We did not have active-duty counterparts in their specialties assigned to PAB. Of course, some of the projects on which the unit worked required more generalized carpentry or masonry skills.

The Air Guard unit acquitted itself admirably on all the projects. FESA again assisted on the electrical upgrade that the hospital desperately needed. A small contingent deployed to Cerro La Mole, and built a small concrete helipad. While there, the contingent also leveled an area near the pad for the local kids to use as a soccer field. Finally, the entire Guard unit had collected old clothes from their communities to bring to the Honduran poor. They distributed their goods to the farm families living on the hills around the site (The few radicals that I have known would no doubt dismiss these humane gestures as nothing more than imperialist whitewash designed to assuage guilty consciences. On the contrary, these were quite genuine acts performed by true citizen soldiers who had braved the barbs and taunts of American "peace" groups protesting their departure from their home airfields).

Most of the carpentry projects came off without a hitch. The new female shower extensions, completed on the main side of base, generally increased morale, as now no one had to adhere to shower schedules. Before, shower hours had rotated between men and women. However, the males did indulge in some rather justifiable grumbling about the relatively large number of shower heads installed compared to the few females on base. The main point of contention, though, one that stretched all the way to SOUTHCOM in Panama, was the installation of a bathtub in the headquarters female shower. One day, I got a call from the Deputy Chief of Staff - Engineer office at Army headquarters in Panama.

"Hey, why the hell did you guys order an eight- hundred-dollar bathtub?"

"Sir, we were ordered to put a bathtub into the headquarters female shower, and that's what a tub costs here in Honduras."

"Who the hell gave you the order?"

"The commander, sir."

A later telephone call informed us that SOUTHCOM had asked the commander about the expenditure. Our commander had confirmed that he had issued the order and further stated that he didn't really care what the tub had cost, because the morale of the women was worth it. The grapevine held that the real reason that a tub was installed only in the headquarters shower, and not in the other female showers, was due to the influence of the female Air Force Lieutenant Colonel serving as PAB's protocol officer. Several of the male soldiers openly entertained briefly the notion of filing a sexual discrimination complaint concerning the shower heads and the tub, but thought better of it upon realizing that the equal opportunity hierarchy (of that time period) was set up more to handle complaints originating with female servicemembers than vice versa. By the time the EO people would have figured out how to handle the complaint, most involved would have returned to the States.

As happened with building bunkers, moving the portable latrines, removing shoddily built do-it-yourself structures, or the bathtub, minor irritants can assume a disproportional importance during deployments, and provide a few moments of mirth or anger.

2 May 1986 PAB

When I arrived here with the Sergeant First Class , he kept commenting on how much PAB looked like a Vietnam-era base camp. I've read innumerable articles and seen many media reports that raise the specter of Vietnam. Even the commander keeps saying that we'll win this one.

The commander I can understand best of all. The Sergeant First Class sees a surface similarity in living conditions. Politicians see that, and a resemblance to the causes and motivations in Vietnam. Yet, the differences are astonishingly blatant. What the commander means is a win on the political front for America, for our military involvement is now too small to be counted for much. Even if we went in for deep military involvement, the odds would be overwhelmingly in our favor, but not without the political powers solidly behind the involvement. What Reagan and the others who deeply care about America's role here must do is show why we are needed, in unambiguous and unimpeachable terms: a media offensive that recognizes and compares Ortega's real achievements with the accomplishments of similar regimes (Fascist Italy, Castro's Cuba, unified Vietnam, Stalin's Soviet Union). We also must show the Contras for what they are. Far more comparison of the Contras with the El Salvadoran guerrillas is necessary. If the FMLN has a right to exist, then so must the Contras. Additionally, we must develop Contra spokesmen, ones who either hold or share power, who are capable of not sounding dogmatic, or bellicose, or merely stupid.

I had a talk with the assistant J-4 [the assistant Logistics officer] tonight. He told me about trying to arrange airlift to feed the new influx of refugees around Mocoron and Rus Rus, most of them Miskito

Indians. I commented on the sorry media coverage of that part of the conflict. He said the refugees were near starvation. As for the airlift, the Government of Honduras did not want to be involved. The U.S. military cannot legally pay such expenses, so the logistics officer was seeking fifteen thousand dollars from the U.S. embassy. Meanwhile, the U.S. citizenry, thanks to our "balanced" media, goes on in its blissful ignorance of yet another minor side effect of the creation of Utopia in Nicaragua. Why do you suppose the relief organizations, church groups, and the United Nations high commissioner are not publicly and loudly demanding aid?

8
MORALE, WELFARE, AND RECREATION

They were the new breed of American regular, who, not liking the service, had insisted, with public support, that the Army be made as much like civilian life and home as possible. Discipline had galled them, and their congressmen had seen to it that it did not become too onerous. They had grown fat.

— T.R. Fehrenbach, *This Kind of War*

9 May 1986 PAB

I've been giving thought to my roots lately. I've always been intrigued by the effect that the sixties had on rural small towns like mine. The movements of the sixties were dominated by the affluent urban kids. So what happened when the affluent urban kids lost their activist zeal and turned to more traditional pursuits - chasing after more money, flashier spouses/mates, bigger and better cars, following the latest trends? Where did the movements leave the kids of humbler origins? What about the rural and small-town kids who, trying to emulate their big-city cousins, revolted, turned on, tuned in, and dropped out? After their audacious attempt to share in a larger youth movement, even if relegated to collateral theaters, what happens when the movement turns out to be only a trend?

George Will said in Statecraft as Soulcraft *that America had counted on her cities in the past to be the repository of civilization, as opposed to the barbaric frontier. I would submit that since the twenties, and in particular, the 1960s, a grand revolution occurred. The cities became more barbaric, and the rural areas held civilization upright.*

Sadly, the urban-led sixties movements directly attacked those civilized values stored in rustic settings. Parental respect and family solidarity became items of ridicule. Close-knit community life became oppressive, stifling. Marriage became bondage. When the urban sickness penetrated to overthrow these pillars of society, what replaced them?

135

Nothing. Now we search in vain for community spirit, for care of illegitimate and abandoned children, for funds to care for dope addicts, for discipline in our schools. In short, we search for what we sought so hard to destroy.

Although it would be exceedingly difficult to make the case that any military, America's included, has been, historically, a repository of clean living, the general decline in formerly traditional values in American society had an effect on its military by the mid-1980s. The war theorist Clausewitz went to some length in his writings to demonstrate how particular kinds of societies throughout history produce particular kinds of militaries, in short, that the military is a reflection of the society from which it springs.

Traditionally, the American soldier saw himself as the defender of home, hearth, and family. Through the defense of his own possessions and values, or of those he hoped to obtain, his sacrifice was extended to his neighbors and to anyone else like himself. But if the bunk-hopping, bunker-banging, and cynical attitudes that went on in Honduras were any indication, too few Americans seemed concerned about such commitments in the 1980s. By then, little had appeared to fill the vacuum left behind.

The decline manifested itself in other ways, too. Certain sections of American intellectual society bellyached for decades that the Cold War militarized American society. Yet the truth is, that with the exception of a few elite units, not even the military was "militarized." As the quote from T.R. Fehrenbach's classic on the Korean War illustrates, this was not a new phenomenon. Maybe we can take comfort in that during peacetime. After Vietnam, American society de-emphasized the patriotic and anything that smacked of the martial spirit. Our recruiting for the all-volunteer force emphasized the educational benefits available, the opportunities for travel and adventure, or the ability to learn a skill before returning to the civilian world. Absent was any suggestion of sacrifice, danger, or nationalism. The commercials and colorful brochures made war seem the continuation of high school sports by other means. At West Point, during my plebe year, we were bombarded with surveys and questionnaires concerning our motivations for joining the Army and attending the Academy. The simple answer, "Because I wanted to serve my country," was nowhere to be found.

In Honduras, certain of these chickens came home to roost. With all the bitching, moaning, and complaining that went on about being deployed for 90 days (for the Air Force) or 180 days (for the Army) to the middle of nowhere with only satellite TV, refrigerators, electricity, USO shows, hot showers, and cold beer for comfort, God help us if we ever again have to live in foxholes. In peacetime, a commander spends much of his time worried about morale. Too often, that morale is defined in terms of gyms, hot rations, booze, swimming pools, etc. The focus, though, is invariably not on what the soldiers have, but on what they lack. They may have all the things we did at PAB, but bitch because they didn't have the racquetball courts that some wanted us to build.

If history is correct, morale is easier to produce with material goods in wartime, even though those goods may be harder to provide. In the chaotic danger and deprivation of war, maybe a hot cup of coffee is all that is necessary to produce good morale. Indeed, if you haven't had one in a while, a mere candy bar can have as much impact as a USO show.

The lessons of Korea and Vietnam also tell us that if we do triumph in our attempts to provide material comfort to the front line, the good life can become distracting and have a deleterious effect on units. The doped-up, drunken Vietnam soldier just back from the bush, getting high in the rear base camp, has passed into Hollywood legend. On one hand, we say we understand. After all, war is hell, and who would begrudge the soldier a little fun, for tomorrow he may die. On the other hand, we wonder how any military organization can function if its members are not of sound mind and body. As dehumanizing as war or military service can be, a soldier has to fight with himself, or should, to stay a civilized human. In Vietnam, although we defeated the enemy time and again, many soldiers lost the war within themselves. In Honduras, we certainly could have done better. Our services and our leaders still frequently emphasized the mind-set of troop morale over values and over training, and sometimes even at the expense of security. I heard one Major General aptly call this phenomena "misplaced compassion"—the kind that will get more of us killed than necessary.

At PAB, the most serious roosting chicken was the attitude

towards security. A soldier-scholar wrote in the late 1980s that "Evidently, the military paid attention . . ." to the lessons of the Iran and Beirut failures. Consequently, "U.S. troops in Honduras have avoided the Marines' mistakes in Lebanon; they routinely guard strong defensive perimeters- in order to frustrate local insurrectionaries."[28] Although I have great respect for this author, I do not know whether he had any firsthand experience in Honduras, but what he described was just not the situation I experienced.

On the contrary, the task force headquarters First Sergeant wisely thought that a roving guard patrol was necessary, given our exposed position and the poor training of the Honduran forces protecting us. You would have thought he had proposed committing mass murder.

"What, me walk patrol? That's crazy, man; I'm a finance clerk ..."

"I'm in the Air Force; we don't do that kind of infantry bullshit, First Sergeant. You Army guys are supposed to protect us. It isn't fair ..."

"What? You mean we have to go down to qualify with our weapon if we're going to patrol? I haven't shot in years ..."

"I didn't join the Army to be sent to some godforsaken place like Honduras to pull no damn guard duty ..."

"Sir, the First Sergeant wants me to pull guard duty. We don't need no damn guards. That's what we got the MPs and Hondos for. You can't let him do this to me."

Sadly, the leadership acquiesced to the unpopularity of the idea. For too many of these soldiers in the supporting branches of the services, the thought of potential combat and the hardships of an austere environment were too much to take.

Many of the misguided efforts at morale-support activities were undertaken to assuage these "blows" to the psyche. Sacrificing and serving is one thing, but couldn't we at least do it in air-conditioned comfort? Out of the horrible bloodletting of the Napoleonic Wars came the belief that in war the moral (meaning the psychological) is to the physical as three is to one. In America, we still say that there are no atheists in a foxhole. What this means is that there is a spiritual dimension to war or military service. But as society has become too sophisticated for spirituality, it is all too easy to let the physical become predominant. The results can approach hedonism.

One day near the end of my tour, I got a call at 0730 hours. The J3 (operations) officer, an Air Force lieutenant colonel, was on the line.
"Captain Waddell, why aren't you over here already? We're about to leave."

"Over where, sir?"

"The flight line, goddamn it! Didn't you get the word last night?"

"No, sir. The word about what?"

"You're going on a recon mission with us today to scout an airstrip."

Now this was something I understood. I had been sent on such missions several times in the past, generally with more warning.

"Should I draw a weapon, sir?"

"No, for chrissake! Just bring a camera and some swim trunks. They didn't tell you anything, did they? We're going to the Bay Islands to scout a possible new R & R location."

Now, I had spent the better part of several days in CH-47 and UH-60 helicopters scouting roads, ports, and airstrips. Honduras had few roads, and Army helicopters were the way to travel. However, refueling requirements were often a pain. Helicopters would lift off, carrying new fuel blivets to replenish the refueling points stuck around the country at places like San Lorenzo or Juticalpa. A long mission might require two or three fuel stops. This was going to be a long mission, for the Bay Islands lay off the northern coast of Honduras.

When I got to the flight line, the J3 filled me in. Evidently, a small planeload of civilians had landed at Palmerola a few days previously, with a group of American businessmen. They had recently bought a small Caribbean island and wanted to turn it into a resort but were having trouble attracting tourists. So, they thought that they might offer some cut-rate R & R deals to the folks at PAB. The commander liked the idea and dispatched two helicopters full of people to take a look. The island had a small airstrip, hence the reason for my inclusion. A couple of people were included because they were known scuba enthusiasts. The provost marshal was sent to check security, and the J3 and the civilian in charge of MWR were sent to report on the overall feasibility. This "mission" consumed hundreds of man-hours and thousands of dollars' worth of aviation fuel. Worse, on the return trip, because of a weather front, our choppers had to set down in the Honduran town of Siguatepeque, where we had to scrounge for lodgings. A whole day and a portion of the next were wasted on this boondoggle.

The only problem with the R & R idea was that the airstrip was unserviceable except for small private planes. That meant a large contingent of U.S. troops could only reach the island by helicopter, a very expensive trip. Yet, upon return, when the staff reported its findings, the concerns were mostly about the availability of booze, cheap scuba equipment, and women (the only one on the island was the paramour of one of the owners). The owners promised to import some attractive locals from the nearby islands to serve as waitresses. What the troops arranged with the girls after hours, they said, was strictly their own business. That settled, the first trip was scheduled for late June or early July—despite the prohibitive cost in man-hours, flight hours, and aviation fuel. This was the outer limit of R & R absurdity.

Yet, the treatment of R & R at PAB followed a well-worn path in the history of American arms. In the Korean War, after the troops had settled into the lines where they would spend most of '52 and '53, R & R in Japan was a short hop away. T. R. Fehrenbach records that "the Americans who passed through Korea and Japan whored and drank with abandon and the whoring and drinking had its chroniclers. Few men wrote of the orphanages supported by battalions."[29] Much the same could have been said of our actions in Honduras, especially as we were at various times accused of such evils as spreading venereal disease and fostering child molestation. Whatever the truth to the bad side of our involvement, the good was often slighted and overshadowed, perhaps because we encouraged, or at least allowed, the seamier side to exist..

As for "luxurious" living in austere surroundings, we also followed a familiar path, with similar results. When the fighting in Korea wound down, senior commanders had little to do but take care of their troops. Heated shelters and mess tents protected the men who did not have to man the line, and commanders began to worry about the trivial, such as the color of name tapes and fire buckets.[30] The soldiers began to get lax, to sleep on patrol. In Vietnam, the troops in base camps had access to "refrigerators, movies, ice cream, PXs, Red Cross girls, air conditioners, tape recorders, their own television and radio stations, free flights to

Asian resort areas, service clubs, Bob Hope Christmas shows, hobby shops, and a host of other fringe benefits. . . . Never in any war has any force been so munificently pampered."[31] The result? "For every man who lived in a grubby bunker on a remote firebase, four or five slept between sheets and, likely as not, in air-conditioned rooms."[32] In Honduras, we had it much better than the Korean vets, but not yet as good as our Vietnam counterparts.

In any case, though, the main forms of recreation were watching TV, drinking, and reading. Hootch A35 had a well-stocked bookshelf when I arrived. It included everything from classic novels to back issues of Hustler. The chaplains also maintained a paperback library. Some of the books I was able to read included *Lines and Shadows* and *Delta Star* by Joseph Wambaugh, *The Sicilian* by Mario Puzo, *The Talisman* by Stephen King and Peter Straub, *Modern Times* by Paul Johnson, *The Haj* by Leon Uris, *The Red Badge of Courage* by Stephen Crane, *Billy Budd* by Herman Melville, *The Hunt for Red October* by Tom Clancy, and *Huckleberry Finn.* I also read *The Death and Life of Dith Pran* by Sydney H. Schanberg, and *The Good War* by Studs Terkel. The last two affected me so much that I recorded my thoughts in the diary.

25 May 1986 PAB

An excerpt from Studs Terkel's The Good War (p. 15) that sums up the often hypocritical definition of right and wrong the United States has lived with for forty-five years. "The crowning irony lay in WWII itself. It had been a different kind of war. 'It was not like other wars,' a radio talk disk jockey reflected aloud. In his banality lay a wild kind of crazy truth. It was not fratricidal. It was not, most of us profoundly believed, 'imperialistic.' Our enemy was, patently, obscene: the Holocaust maker. It was one war that many who would have resisted 'your other wars' supported enthusiastically. It was a 'just war," if there is any such animal."

Yet, despite Terkel's meanderings, World War II was much like previous nationalistic wars up to the point that we learned of the Holocaust and could use it as a motivator, i.e., very late in the conflict.

"Just War?" We fought with an ally, Stalin, who was as obscenely murderous as Hitler, one who actually began the war in conjunction

with Hitler.

What Terkel implies is that World War II was a crusade against evil. But, in justifying this crusade against fascism, based on the evidence of aggression and the Holocaust, he opens the door to justify other crusades, especially against the Left, the only real peddlers of aggression, mass exile, and mass murder nowadays. Yet, to Terkel and the others of his ilk, for the United States to stand up to such actions from the Left, as we are trying to do here at PAB, would, I'm sure, be one of "your other wars" in the "imperialistic" mode. That's where the hypocrisy comes in.

26 May 1986 PAB Memorial Day
An appropriate thought for the day: Blessed are the peacemakers, for they shall be called the children of God.

I hope God sees peacemakers in those of us who wear uniforms for the sake of deterring war.

8 June 1986 PAB
I'm now living with a Samoan captain, a Puerto Rican captain, a half-Nisei lieutenant, a Chinese captain of the USAF Civil Engineering, and a German captain of the USAF Air Weather Service. Ain't the U.S. Army and joint operations something?

One of the finest people I have ever known now lived in the hootch. He was a Captain and a USAF Civil Engineer. He had been born in the hill communities outside of the city of Hong Kong. His family farmed a small plot of land until they immigrated to America when the Captain was six. He grew up in New York City. Like millions before them, this family grabbed onto the American dream. They didn't find the streets paved with gold, only with opportunity. All of his siblings had graduated from college. The Captain himself graduated from the prestigious engineering school at Columbia University. His father still worked in a Chinese laundry. The Captain was a devout Catholic and dedicated soldier. Having people like him in the service could make one think that all was right with the world.

If some of the people assigned to Palmerola were truly lost men, like Mad Mike, there were also a few who became rejuvenated by serving in Honduras. Most of them were old veterans on their last tours before retirement, and someone had sent them to Honduras, maybe as a joke, maybe just to get rid of a member of the ROAD crew—Retired On Active Duty. Honduran service gave them a chance to be useful again, gave them some power, and maybe a little excitement that was missing from their desk jobs back home.

Captain R was one of these. He was, like Mad Mike, a captain with nearly eighteen year's time-in- grade in the Air Force. He had not been promoted despite having served well as a crewmember on aircraft, in the missile silos, and now in intelligence. Yet Honduras seemed a tonic for him. He came in cynical and surly, but got into the job of keeping track of the various bad guys in Central America.

Another example was an aviator who claimed to have been one of the president's helicopter pilots. Although he had been promoted well enough, he had had no shot at a unit command, and he was considered too old for other interesting jobs. His service wanted younger blood. So, he was sent to Honduras. He took over the J3 section and ran it with a good deal of wry, sarcastic humor, but also with a lot of insight and energy. He also got into better shape and regained the gravity one expected of a man of his rank and responsibility. Still, his favorite saying when someone came in demanding an immediate response to something trivial was, "What? Are the Russians already in the motor pool?" Palmerola affected different people in different ways.

9 June 1986 PAB

Lieutenant G, a portly, fair-skinned fellow, arrived today from Fort Carson. He came to replace my Lieutenant.

Lieutenant G quickly succumbed to PAB life. My Lieutenant immediately took to showing him the ropes of the job. Somewhere, though, Lieutenant G got hold of some bad local food. Within three days of arrival, he was flat on his back in the hospital with a severe case of dysentery. It took a week for him to recover.

Shortly after G's arrival, the Engineer section went to Tela Beach on the Honduran Caribbean coast for an MWR beach party. The resort was run-down, but with the right development, it could have been an attractive tourist destination. Eventually, it would gain some notoriety for hosting a conference of all the Central American presidents, where the duplicitous but shrewd diplomacy of Daniel Ortega, combined with the simple-minded do-goodism of Oscar Arias and the partisan politics of certain U.S. politicians, seemed to undermine much of the U.S. efforts of the entire decade. The mantra was "give peace a chance" which when translated into plain English apparently meant, "Give the Sandinistas and the FMLN a few more chances." Despite the additional chances, both leftwing groups failed in their designs for violent revolution as their main patron, the Soviets, collapsed, and their opponents remained persistent.

The regular morale support weekends were paid for with taxpayer funds. The government provided transportation and rooms. The service member only had to pay for his drinks and food. The government was picking up our transportation (a rented vehicle) and our lodgings (a beach house). This was an R & R weekend on the cheap, though. We had raided the small PX before we left, buying all the hot dogs and beer we could. A case of MREs with their vacuum-packed and dehydrated main courses rounded out our gourmet menu.

The ride up to Tela was one beer-soaked adventure. Soon after checking in, we hit the beach. That evening, some of the team arranged feminine companionship. Fear of disease, lack of money, fatigue, or some other lame excuse was often the reason given for not participating in Honduras' tropic delights. It just wasn't cool to admit that fidelity might guide one's actions.

Aside from any personal values, another good reason to avoid prostitutes was the likely damage to U.S.- Honduran relations. One of the common complaints about U.S. forces anywhere in the world is the increase in sleaze that they bring with them. Honduras was no exception. One could easily pick up the looks of disdain from the local citizens as they saw our little group. Even the whores did not seem particularly appreciative of the business. However, they did appreciate the food. The women ate all the food we had brought, even the dehydrated MREs. I did not know the compensation negotiated between the customers and the women, but money must have been only a part.

We bumped into a group of Peace Corps workers who were at Tela on a similar trip. We exchanged mutual pleasantries, and then got down to a game of one-upmanship in Third World development. Most of them were English teachers and had been plying their trade. When asked what we were doing in the country, we could confidently reply that we had been drilling wells, building roads and schoolhouses, and other projects of direct benefit to the populace. They suspected us, it seemed, of being CIA or Green Berets, or some other denizen of the dark forces of American imperialism. They did accuse the American forces, quite correctly, of luring young Honduran women into prostitution. If they had only known.

I realize that my participation on the trips opens me to the charge of hypocrisy. So be it, but my MWR trips to Copan and Tela convinced me that these excursions presented more trouble than they were worth. The Americans on the trips were totally isolated, unarmed, and at the mercy of any renegade, terrorist, or rebel. A couple of years after my tour, one of the trip buses was indeed attacked with gunfire. Additionally, the trips gave too much opportunity for ugly Americanism, unintentional or not. Large, loud, heavy-drinking foreigners flashing wads of money in generally poor surroundings would scarcely be welcomed anywhere. The tours of duty at PAB were so short that the need for the trips was doubtful. If the command felt that they were essential for morale, some arrangement should have been made for the trips to be taken out of the country, but not necessarily at some outrageously expensive island resort as was proposed for the private island. We had military aircraft flying in every day that could have taken troops back Stateside for a few days. The gain in public relations with the Hondurans surely would have offset any anger from the Honduran resorts involved.

As to the general point of whether the average level of morale was high enough to allow us to do our jobs well, a noted sociologist, Charles Moskos had visited PAB sometime in the previous year, when conditions had been even more primitive, and noted:

> "The morale and commitment of the American soldiers in Honduras, male and female alike were remarkably high. Although few of the GIs had any strategic or geopolitical sense of the American presence in Honduras, they considered their work

important in terms of immediate and short-range duty requirements. Considering the Spartan living conditions and arduous work, the good spirits of the soldiers were striking."[33]

Morale, like the Honduran weather, blew hot and cold.

9
THE ADVERSARIAL RELATIONSHIP

On one of these six Cold Harbor days, when my battery was in action, I saw a party of horsemen riding towards us from the left. I smiled as the absurdity of men riding along a battle-line for pleasure filled my sense of the ridiculous; but as I looked I saw that the party consisted of a civilian under escort. The party passed close behind our guns, and in passing the civilian exposed a large placard, which was fastened to his back, and which bore the words, "Libeller of the Press". We all agreed that he had been guilty of some dreadful deed, and were pleased to see him ride the battle-line. He was howled at, and the wish to tear him limb from limb and strew him over the ground was fiercely expressed.

— From the recordings of Frank Wilkerson, Union soldier; Max
     Hastings, ed, *The Oxford Book of Military Anecdotes*

22 June 1986 PAB
Reflections on reading The Death and Life of Dith Pran:

Schanberg states (p. 15) that he and Dith Pran believed, devoutly wished and hoped, that the Khmer Rouge would end the killing once the nasty ol' Americans left Cambodia. That turned out to be no more likely than the congressional liberals' hopes that the North Vietnamese would seek a coalition government once President Thieu of South Vietnam resigned.

As for the extent of U.S. aid to the communist cause in Southeast Asia, Schanberg reports (p. 25) that in front of the former Information Ministry, after he was released from accidental captivity, a Khmer official, Schanberg believed to be a general, addressed a group of international newsmen. The official volunteered "our thanks to the

147

American people, who have helped us from the beginning."

In *Our Great Spring Victory* by the North Vietnamese general, Dung, one finds similar expressions of thanks to the more "progressive" elements of American society.[34] It is well known that some of the antiwar leaders in the sixties met with representatives of the Viet Cong and North Vietnamese to find out what might best serve the interests of the Communists.[35] Now, I am not suggesting conspiracy in any way, since these meetings often happened quite openly, and were recorded and publicized at the time. The Communists well understood that anything that weakened the resolve of the United States to continue its military efforts in Southeast Asia worked to their advantage. If the Communists had to expend little or no effort to encourage domestic U.S. opposition, so much the better. In the end, though, our demonstrators became the unwitting allies of our adversaries, as did any journalist who sought to expose the workings of legitimate military operations with which they disagreed, or any journalist, public figure, or other opinion-maker that consciously chose to sympathize with the Communist cause. That our society gave those sympathizers, or their more benign comrades—those who did not sympathize with the Communists, but merely sought an end to U.S. involvement in a "futile war," or in a morally ambiguous conflict—an open platform for their views is heartening, to say the least, to anyone who professes a love of democracy. Whether these people were willing tools, or just useful fools, the effect on our national resolve was the same. Such is the price of American domestic democracy, and one we must remain willing to pay time and again.

The general perception in the military that still lingered in the mid-1980s about the media being openly against the Vietnam war, a press that should have remain balanced except on the Op-Ed page, was disquieting. Evidence existed to perpetuate this perception. Schanberg still maintained that we Americans were looking for "something positive out of the darkness of that period" (p. 75). He tells of a former serviceman who wrote "and for you, Mr. Dith, I am truly sorry and hope you can forgive me and those who served with me for what we have done" (p. 75). For Schanberg, the fundamental fact of life for the Cambodians remains what it has been since 1970: "their fate and future are in control of others and their condition is tragedy." These views dovetail nicely with the Schanberg character's most memorable line in the film version of *The Killing Fields*. Upon winning the Pulitzer Prize, the Schanberg character is asked by a fellow journalist if he feels any responsibility for the Cambodian slaughter as a possible result of his reporting from there. The character deftly parries any personal responsibility, while simultaneously absolving the Khmer Rouge by blaming the entire Cambodian calamity on the insanity produced by $7 billion of illegal U.S. bombing. Schanberg refused, and still does, to see himself as one of those "others" that however briefly controlled the destiny of Cambodia.

The truth is that the Cambodians were the primary instrument of their own destruction. They allowed the North Vietnamese to use up to a third of their country as a safe haven and a conduit for the Communist war effort in Vietnam. Then, in response to the growing control being exercised by Cambodia's ancient ethnic enemies, Lon Nol took over the Cambodian government and asked for U.S. assistance in fighting the Communists. In response, the North Vietnamese created the Khmer Rouge. Of course, the Khmer Rouge were Cambodians and, when they won, had total control of that country's destiny. The Khmer performance while in power cannot be blamed on anybody but themselves, their benefactors, and their perverted communist ideology.

28 June 1986 PAB

Playboy, June 1986, "Smack in the Middle of a Low-Intensity Conflict" by Asa Barber. Barber is an early sixties Marine veteran of Vietnam. His article is full of clichés and serves as a good example of the free-lance journalism on the subject of CENTAM's conflicts. He traveled with a group of Americans that visited El Salvador, Honduras, and Nicaragua all within ten days.

"This is a country [Nicaragua] at war with our surrogates, the contras, but I will not find a veteran in the delegation who thinks Nicaragua is a military threat to the United States." (p. 192)

Also on page 192, Barber describes an El Salvadoran colonel as frank, blunt, embarrassed. This description is counterpoised with a description of a Sandinista colonel as handsome, soft-spoken, and possessing "immense professionalism."

"Nicaragua must embrace raw capitalism and nothing else or we [Americans] will squeeze it like a lemon, kill its children, invade its borders and snuff out the flames." (p. 194)

"Honduras ... is essentially a client state of the United States." (p. 194)

The Contra leader "rants like a maniac, venom spewing." (p. 195)

During a meeting between Barber's group and the Contras: "The contras are proving to us that they are what their critics say they are: former Somoza National Guardsmen, former death-squad members, hit men, and rogues." (p. 195)

To Barber it appears likely "the U.S. will invade Nicaragua before the current administration leaves office. ... It will be Reagan's parting gift to his more conservative followers" (p. 197)

The worst Barber ever says about the Communists: "The Sandinistas are not angels ..."

This sort of rhetoric appears in the media daily under the guise of reporting. Perhaps the Nick Nolte film, Under Fire, *and the recent* Salvador *by Oliver Stone tell us more about activist journalists than the media would care to admit.*

30 June 1986 PAB
Who decides that the public is to receive daily dosages of consciousness-raising about South Africa? Who decides that the public doesn't get equal doses about Afghanistan, Angola, the darker side of the Sandinistas? Who decides to concentrate on alleged human- rights abuses by the Contras while glossing over those of the Sandinistas? Who decides to portray Marcos's police hosing down demonstrators as "political repression," which undoubtedly it is, but portrays Aquino's hosing of demonstrators as mere "disturbances"?

Our popular perception today of twentieth century evil is flawed. Nazi Germany and America in Vietnam are the linchpins of the perception, but where are communism and its horrors?

When I read these diary records, I am as surprised at my bitterness toward the media as I was at my bitterness towards the anti-involvement or pro-Sandinista activists. Nonetheless, the entries are an accurate reflection not only of my feelings, but of most of those with whom I served. The relationship between the military and the media was always tense.

One evening after finishing my duties, I strolled up the brick walkway towards A35, my hootch. As I passed the bohio, a covered patio that served as Joint Task Force-Bravo's common meeting place, I observed what could be described as a metaphor for the state of military-media relations in the mid-1980s. The task force commander faced about a dozen men and women clad in civilian clothes, cameras and tape recorders dangling from their bodies, notebooks in their hands. The commander was alone and looked quite anxious, uncomfortable, out of place, maybe even fearful, which was quite unusual for him. When I tuned into the conversation, I understood why. The commander was patiently explaining in unclassified terms exactly what the small American force then operating in Honduras was trying to accomplish. The journalists kept shouting questions and challenges at him about the effectiveness of the ongoing training exercises and about alleged ties to the Contras. Perhaps most disconcerting was the fellow who shouted, "Why should we believe you?" In a nutshell, here was the adversarial relationship between an agent of government and the agents of the free press.

Put in terms less stark than that of the patio confrontation, this adversarial relationship is quite complex. The very essence of the media is information. A journalist's elemental existence involves the gathering and reporting of data. Yet, to the military, information is simultaneously a tool, a weapon, and a threat. Members of the media did not really trust those wearing uniforms, perhaps especially those military stage managers called public affairs officers (PAOs). Hence, the press sought out the highest ranking or the most involved for the truly definitive account. Conversely, PAOs were created precisely to relieve the burden on troop leaders imposed by having to deal with large numbers of journalists. The emotional baggage of the Vietnam War, handed down informally to the new generation of soldiers, made it hard for those in uniform to view the approach of a camera-toter with feelings other than apprehension. Yet, the relationship was strangely symbiotic.

The average American was a member of the information age even in the 1980s before the advent of the internet, especially servicemen who were hungry for any scrap of news from home. The portable transistor radios that blared over the battlefields of Vietnam had been replaced by the Walkman and its clones. At Palmerola Air Base, almost all the shacks had a color TV hooked into the Armed Forces Radio and Television System, where one could pick up the bland, amateurish productions and re-runs befitting a government enterprise. Thankfully, though, the major units operating at Palmerola had purchased a bevy of satellite dishes that allowed us to pick up the cable movie channels, CNN (then the only cable news channel widely offered), and a few local stations broadcasting in the southern states. The Miami Herald and USA Today would sometimes arrive only a day or two old. Many individuals had their newsmagazine subscriptions routed to Central America, too. Consequently, we were as plugged in to the mainstream of print and broadcast journalism as one could be in Honduras. Being an observer of and participant in the events so often depicted had an eerie quality all its own.

Servicemen depended on the media as a vital lifeline to all that we considered precious and worth defending. But the media also depended on us for much of its livelihood when crises developed. Of course, journalists looked for the official or unattributed source, but more fundamentally, they depend on the military for access to the area of operations, and for protection once there. Perhaps we soldiers were looking for a bunch of Ernie Pyles, and maybe the journalists, too, were looking for the reverence and access they had in World War II, while simultaneously maintaining their fealty to the cynicism that had become the media's daily bottom line. Neither group was satisfied; I often heard expressed, often with a sigh, the sentiment that "it is a good thing today's media wasn't present at the Battle of the Bulge, or Hitler might have won ..."

During the Sandinista border incursion of March 1986, one of the few helicopters we had at our disposal was put to the task of transporting loads of journalists to the conflict, and then getting them back in time to file their stories. I've already related the story above of the unauthorized journalist whom we stranded in Miskitia. Sometimes the journalists got housed and fed by American forces. At what cost do we subsidize the free press? Who repays the government for the cost of helicopter and airplane rides? American servicemen had to pay for the rations they ate; did journalists? What was the operational cost of jerking a helicopter or airplane out of service in order to maintain good media relations?

This brings up another disturbing question, one that hits close to the heart of the adversarial relationship. During the same border incident, most news agencies were able to send reporters to both sides. On the evening news, the journalists would duly report the information provided by the task force. However, their statements were always tempered with prefaces such as "The Reagan administration contends . . ."; "Those running the show here in Honduras maintain . . . but we have not been able to obtain independent confirmation of the information provided." Then the report would shoot off to Tegucigalpa where a single member of the Honduran opposition would be presented as a dissenter from the official line, "Not everyone in the Honduran Government agrees ..." Yet, when the cameras turned to the Sandinistas, a subtle shift in wording occurred, "The Nicaraguan government reports ..." with no attempt to find a Nicaraguan opposition politician and no comments questioning the veracity of the information. The thrust, at least to this observer, was that the information supplied by our government was somehow less credible than that supplied by the other side. In other words, only American assertions, especially those supplied by the military, had to be independently confirmed.

I can remember watching a CNN broadcast one evening, and being quite startled when I realized that it had been filmed right outside my hut. That "on-location" quality was the only similarity between the situation presented and that, which really had occurred. The reporter was saying something about us contending that about two hundred Sandinistas had been killed or injured in the fighting, but that this reporter had seen no more than five bodies purported to be from Nicaragua. During our daily intelligence briefings, we were giving ourselves the same casualty totals. I felt insulted, not only because the reporter naturally assumed that she had been lied to but also due to the journalistic implication that we soldiers were so stupid and incompetent that we had to be lying to ourselves. Perhaps the media has been given inaccurate, exaggerated, or incomplete figures by the U.S. government in the past; perhaps journalistic training requires corroboration to the extent possible, but when the members of the media assume that they will always be lied to, or in searching for balance, they accept the flimsiest data from contending viewpoints, servicemen will react by holding all members of their profession in contempt and will actively avoid contact with them. The results? Even less of the true story gets out. Journalists take righteous umbrage when members of the military question their loyalty, patriotism, and good sense. So why do the journalists have so few qualms about questioning the integrity and technical competence of soldiers every chance they get?

All of these anti-media feelings were fed and flamed by the low level of competency or lack of fidelity to detail that was too often present in military-affairs reporting. One of the dust-covered magazines hanging around in the corners of the Engineer office was an edition of *Common Cause* from September/October 1984.[36] The author of an article on the U.S. involvement in Honduras, Jacqueline Sharkey, insinuated that we had been mothballing air bases all over Honduras in case of war with Nicaragua. If she had ever visited any of these "bases," she would have known how ludicrous her assertion was. The rains quickly washed out the dirt strips our exercises had built, and any of the hootches left unattended quickly deteriorated in the tropical climate. Hell, even the ones we were trying to maintain full-time at PAB were going fast.

In the 2 June 1986 issue of *U. S. News and World Report* an article appeared that described PAB as being a "large tent city near a runaway."[37] The piece also described C-130 cargo planes taking off from PAB "as they rise slowly above the lushness of deep-green forest." Still further in the article, the author contended that the U.S. troops sent to Honduras were "being schooled in the ways of jungle warfare." However, just like Sharkey, I wonder if the authors of this article had ever been to Honduras. If they had, it is hard to believe that they actually went to PAB, which is situated in a broad, agricultural valley almost devoid of forest cover, except for a few pine and banana trees. At the time of the article, almost all of PAB was housed in hootches, not tents, and only a few of the troops ever training in Honduras at the time actually got into the real jungle of the north and the northeast of the country. Why? Partly because there were so few facilities in that part of the country to handle large numbers of American soldiers. Also, the Sandinistas were most likely to come, if they ever did, through the drier, more open regions of the southwest.

Then, on June 30, 1986, *Newsweek* ran an article on "A Big Brother for Honduras."[38] Guess who? The point of this article was that the U.S. presence had taken on a "permanent air." The evidence adduced was the fact that some of the hootches had been converted to recreational clubs and a cinema (which the article failed to mention served mainly as the chapel). Also, the article continued, we had cable TV! Most disconcerting was the photo appearing with the article: a picture of one of Comayagua's prostitutes with the caption "Hearts and Minds?" Although these writers had definitely been to PAB and Comayagua, they were evidently far more impressed with the cable TV and the crumbling hootches selling PX beer than we were.

My favorite article, though, appeared in the *Atlanta Constitution* on 27 February 1986, written by syndicated columnist Richard Reeves. The thesis was that "There is a military coup of sorts going on in Honduras ... It is a move by the American military against the government in Washington." Reeves contended that we soldiers felt free to "ignore and evade" the law by cooking the figures on construction in Honduras. His evidence? A GAO report that detailed some accounting errors. He also objected to "temporary" as a description, contending, with the GAO, that we intended to stay. Hence, "The military was, in other words, lying from the beginning ..." The rest of the article is full of the "obvious deceptions" that led to the "sneaky militarization of poor little Honduras ..." Yet Reeves almost expresses surprise at one point that the military "considers itself in an adversarial relationship" with the press. In retrospect, given the very small numbers of troops and funds involved in Honduras since the mid-1980s, such writing comes across as even more laughable now than it did when originally published.

The GAO—the Government Accountability Office—is, the self-described "investigative arm of Congress," or the "congressional watchdog."[39] Irate congressmen and senators send the GAO to investigate not only the profligate, but also the politically unpopular. As long as federal money is involved, there is no limit to what they can look into. Despite its requirement to be "objective, fact-based, nonpartisan, nonideological, fair, and balanced," given the politically-charged topics the GAO is sent to investigate, the agency sometimes appears as a political tool, rather than a mere budgetary and accounting research aid. GAO reports occasionally come across as passionate political statements, depending on the topic, the congressional investigating committees, and the characterizations of their findings by the media. It is often too easy for critics to infer underhanded political motives from accounting errors. The federal accounting requirements are numerous, often confusing, and sometimes conflicting. Only an expert, like those at GAO, could be expected to comply completely with the letter of the laws. Yet those of us who were Richard Reeves' liars and coupmongers who were allegedly ignoring and evading the law while serving in Honduras were neither experts, nor did we serve in our positions long enough to develop the needed expertise. We were not allowed longer tours because longer tours might have meant we were "operating" rather than "training," or that we had become "permanent" rather than "temporary."

To imply that a coup was taking place is preposterous. Even intentional accounting errors like those alluded to by Reeves would require an enormous conspiracy of hundreds of people, most of whom had never seen or talked to one another, stretching over the length of our involvement in Honduras. The sheer numbers of generals, congressmen and their aides, and journalists who came to PAB to be briefed on this very topic, and the regularly required reports submitted by PAB's engineer, contracting, and budget offices that detailed our actions belie the whole notion of subterfuge. I'm not a syndicated columnist, but I can figure that out.

So much of the story of what was going on in Central America was poorly reported or not reported at all. America had militarized Honduras, as the story went, but with a force that, on any given day, except for the few big exercises of short duration, was smaller than the British force in Belize, or the Soviet-Cuban force in Nicaragua. Cuban pilots flying Sandinista gunships into action got scant coverage. Soviet-financed, Cuban-built airfields and naval bases in Nicaragua never excited as much journalistic interest as the dirt strips "mothballed" in Honduras.

Although the Reagan administration's constant contention that the Sandinistas were arming the FMLN in El Salvador was generally greeted with skepticism in our media, when arms shipments or arms caches were found, little or nothing appeared in the papers or on TV. Volumes were written and hours of broadcast time were devoted to the problems of the Contras in Honduras, but the El Salvadoran encampments in Honduras that served as a safe haven for FMLN rebels and their families along the southern Honduran border were hardly if ever noted by journalists. The notion that the American military, whatever its failings might be dedicated, generally competent, and respectful of the law, escaped the media mentality.

The media maintained that it could not trust the military because the military and the government lied about Vietnam. On the other hand, journalists will tell you that there is absolutely no reason why journalists cannot be trusted with sensitive operational information—indeed, most war correspondents will cite instances when they personally withheld information that they thought might be damaging to the troops doing the fighting. What seems to escape the journalistic mind, though, is that if a journalist cannot trust the military because of Vietnam, then there is also very little reason for a soldier to trust a journalist, because the press in Vietnam, in the opinion of many serving in the mid-1980s, had often been openly hostile to the military, emphasizing the negative, and distorting the facts. Also, it ought to appear incredible to the average American that journalists want the security of our military secrets to depend on the good judgment and conscience of professionals who get fame and fortune from breaking news stories ahead of the competition. Soldiers and government civilians who work with secret material have to be vetted to do so. Often journalists and their crews of technicians are not even American citizens, and they certainly are not subjected to the same level of vetting.

Media personalities of the 1980s concerned with the military-media relationship normally invoked the First Amendment's protection of a free press to justify their actions. They also cited instances of journalistic reports having salutary effects on foreign and military policy. Often cited was the impact of William Howard Russell, whose reports of the conditions of British troops in the Crimean War helped to topple the British government of the day. Yet nothing in the Constitution requires instantaneous reporting. Certainly, Russell's accounts took many days—if not weeks—to reach the British home press. But what was demanded in the 1980s was up-close, instantaneous coverage of military events so that the dramatic footage could be on cable news almost as it occurred. Failing that, it needed to be available for the prime-time nightly news. If this rapidity and visual drama were denied, the normal contention went, the government would be able to cover up flaws, and the American people would not be able to adequately judge their elected officials. However, when so many people are involved, as with any large military operation, the story behind any wrongdoing will always get out, but it might not get out in time for the evening news. Even so, when such a story gets out, we shouldn't expect its tardy nature to have any less effect than Russell's tardy dispatches did, or indeed, any of the bulk of such news coverage prior to the advent of TV and the internet.

The First Amendment also does not require the reporters of private, profit-making enterprises be given access to sensitive operations every time they demand it. Perhaps, though, the military had learned this lesson well since Vietnam. Reporters were largely shut out of the Grenada operation. Due to the outrage this provoked among the media, the Department of Defense agreed to create a press pool where a certain number of reporters from the print and broadcast media would stay on standby for any future Grenada-style operation, or to cover other hard-to-reach operations. The pool was deployed several times successfully, most notably to the Persian Gulf naval mission to escort Kuwaiti tankers during the Iran-Iraq War. But when JUST CAUSE happened in December 1989, several flaws arose with the pool.

First, the standby arrangements worked poorly. The media establishments had difficulty finding their staff, as the operation occurred after normal business hours near the Christmas holidays. Indeed, only one of the reporters who showed up had any experience as a war correspondent. As for security, *Time* magazine staffers openly discussed the pool's call-out at a Christmas party of over two hundred people. When the pool did arrive in Panama, it arrived several hours after the main fighting was over. This caused the greatest anger among the pool participants, but since the initial assault was made by parachute, and the correspondents' arrival had to await the securing of the airfield, little could have been done.

Nonetheless, media outrage prompted the Department of Defense to do yet another study on how the military had mistreated the media. It hired a former war correspondent, Fred Hoffman, to do the report. Not surprisingly, the report blamed the military for "excessive secrecy." Hoffman also complained about the military's inadequate supply of fax machines, transportation, and communication facilities to get the stories rapidly back home.

Indeed the report recommended, and the Defense Department accepted in principle, that "necessary resources, such as helicopters, ground vehicles, communications equipment, etc., must be earmarked specifically for pool use, that the pool must have access to the earliest action . . . "[40] It seems the media did not want just to be "free," but also subsidized and protected. The Hoffman report did not mention the effect that earmarking such equipment might have on the operational capabilities of commanders involved in the earliest actions, nor did it mention anything about the safety of American soldiers who would be assigned to drive, fly, or protect correspondents, their equipment, and their dramatic footage as the pool flitted about the battlefield.

I note with no small amount of satisfaction that the military imposed quite strenuous controls over the media in both Operations Desert Shield and Desert Storm, and the public supported those measures with massive approval ratings. With reporters and reports like the ones above, it's a wonder the military-media relationship did not degenerate from being merely adversarial into open conflict.

10
GOING HOME

In my value system what is being done in Nicaragua is as follows: a man named Ronald Reagan is sending a group of hired thugs to murder, rape, and terrorize women and children who have done nothing to him and who are trying to live ordinary lives in a small country two thousand miles from where Reagan is daily barbered, fed, doctored, helicoptered, televised when he lies about what he is doing to the Nicaraguans, and generally treated—quite wrongly—as a sane and responsible human being who at heart is really a very nice guy.

What Captain Waddell is doing is helping Reagan's thugs. No doubt he is a highly educated, intelligent, and morally admirable person in familial and social relations in our country. He is, however, sent to Honduras as part of Reagan's direct assistance to paid assassins, torturers, rapists, looters, destroyers of medical treatment and supplies to sick and wounded people in a country with which we are not at war . . .

In each age there is invented an Enemy: a subhuman and cunning devil, a legitimate prey, a source of wealth for the enterprising, a reason why we can empty the jails as was done in medieval England to find soldiers enough, and let those who have been outlaws and thieves in their own country go and practice their arts with official sanction against the Enemy . . .

> — Carter Revard, Rhodes Scholar, 1952, in a reply to my letter to the *American Oxonian* (cited at the beginning of Chapter 4)

2 July 1986, 1540 hours, New Orleans Airport

Reflections on the one hundredth birthday of the Statue of Liberty. A new statue should be erected somewhere along the Rio Grande at night, using illegal labor paid one dollar an hour. Call it the Statue of Last Refuge.

160

The logo that should be inscribed, preferably in Spanish, is:
     "Give me your poor, your tired, your huddled masses yearning to be service industry workers, drug smugglers, welfare recipients, and Democrat block voters. Follow the gleam of my lamp of shame as I lift it beside this muddy stream."

As I have said previously, after only a few months in Honduras we tended to become overly cynical. Some of the proponents of U.S. policy in this period utilized the fear of a flood of refugees fleeing from Central American instability as a means of arguing for maintaining or expanding U.S. efforts. Indeed, the approximately one million Cubans and the several hundred thousand Central American refugees that the United States had absorbed in the first 25 years after the rise of Fidel Castro served as a clear indicator of the validity of this concern.

That America accepted so many of these victims is surely laudable, as is the fact that the vast majority of them made decent lives for themselves here. On the other hand, that we have not always accepted them willingly or well suggests how far we as a society have still to go. As my diary entry mentions, large numbers of immigrants were crossing the border daily in the mid-80s despite the risks involved, despite the poverty, mistreatment and political exploitation that too often awaited them.

In November 1986, a few months after my return from Honduras, the U.S. "fixed" the problem of illegal immigration by passing the Immigration Reform and Control Act of 1986. The Act encompassed new sanctions on any employers that did not make a good faith effort to verify the legal status of their employees, enhanced immigration enforcement, and offered amnesty for illegal aliens that could demonstrate they had lived in the U.S. continuously since before 1982. Upon signing the Act, President Reagan said it was comprehensive, stating, "The employer sanctions program is the keystone and major element. It will remove the incentive for illegal immigration by eliminating the job opportunities which draw illegal aliens here."[41] About 2.7 million received amnesty under the program. However, within a few years, the Act had clearly failed. The employer sanctions provisions were undermined by widespread document fraud. Moreover, illegal immigration surged to between 500,000-800,000 per year in the 15 years after the law's passage, and largely in the absence of the insurgencies and political instability roundly blamed for the immigration in the 1980s. The promised enhanced enforcement was never fully implemented – in the first decade after passage, the Federal government deported a cumulative total of only 335,000. Instead, the Federal Immigration and Naturalization Service simply handed out 1.3 million additional "green cards" to illegal immigrants on top of the 2.7 million directly benefited by the 1986 amnesty. As in previous immigration reforms in 1952 and 1965, the 1986 Act brought unintended consequences that dwarfed the original intent. By 2000, Congress was considering a new "comprehensive reform" to the previous comprehensive reform, again promising some form of employer sanctions and enhanced enforcement, coupled once again with a widespread amnesty.[42] A decade later, with an estimated 12 million illegal immigrants in the U.S., the debate continues and still rankles.

The powerful mitigation of the pessimism of this diary entry is that the long-run opportunities of the American experience have always overcome the immediate shortcomings. The people of Central America and the U.S. taxpayers both deserved better than they have received. The question for policy makers, 25 years later, still turns on whether it is better to work on improving the conditions within Mexico and Central America while enhancing our border controls, or just ignoring those conditions and focusing our efforts on aiding the lucky few who make it to America, or pursuing some policy which is a combination of the two. Another strategic consequence of this immigration – both legal and illegal – is that remittances of U.S. wages to home countries now dwarfs all forms of official aid. By 2007, immigrants were sending abroad $42.2 billion that they had earned in the U.S. economy, mostly to Mexico and Central America. For Mexico alone, this is $25 billion per year, and is the second largest source of foreign currency after the export of oil.[43] Radical changes to immigration or remittance policies would have to take into account the likely negative economic effects in the developing countries. Given that nations do not ignore the plight of their neighbors for long, any solution will require balancing compassion with the need to avoid rewarding law breaking. To be truly effective, though, any new comprehensive reform would require effective execution and be flexible enough to adapt to the almost inevitable unintended consequences. A tall order, given the record of policy failure so far.

3 July 1986, Ft Lewis, Washington

Got in about 2330 hours last night. Very nice to be home. I felt like the Pope in that I wanted to fall to my knees and kiss the ground of America.

Nothing fascinating on the return trip except for the following two items. Three times as many aliens as American citizens got off the plane in New Orleans, but they were through immigration before we were.

At the customs stop in New Orleans, the baggage checker and I had the following conversation.

"So, you were in Honduras? Are we doing any good down there?" he asked.

"I think so."

"Did you get to shoot anybody?"

"No, thank God. I didn't want to shoot anybody. We just put in some wells, a school house, and some other projects—you know ..."

I didn't belabor the point that we had built an airfield, a heliport, etc. He wouldn't have understood.

Going home. What could be more pleasing to a serviceman? The feeling starts several days before the actual travel date. The anticipation develops into almost palpable tastes, sounds, smells of the ultimate destination until the anxiety is close to unbearable. The soldiers' talk is a queer mixture of cynicism about what they have done and those they have met, but also of the pride that only comes from hard work and sacrifice.

You can tell when a soldier or a group of them are "short." Even the dourest develop an exuberance that at times can verge on manic joviality. They walk continuously, never still, and talk incessantly, especially about what they'll do when they first arrive. All thoughts turn to leaving.

I envisioned every aspect of the departure and travel for several days, from the leaving of my billets for the last time, catching the ride to the airport, waiting in the terminal, boarding and takeoff. All is merely prelude, though, to arriving.

I mentally walk myself off the plane and into the arms of my wife. Or, if she can't make it to the airport, I see myself arriving at home's front door. I see my wife opening the door. Then begins a million words flowing in a torrent of stored up conversations. Is there anything more special to a serviceman than going home? Yes, arriving.

EPILOGUE

We must remember that one man is much the same as another, and that he is best who is trained in the severest school.
— Thucydides, History of the Peloponnesian War.

Well, we don't have to practice being miserable. It comes naturally.
— A common barracks saying.

As the diary accounts above tied into the mosaic of on-going events in America and the world, so did the pattern of U.S. actions in Central America. By at least one count, since World War II until 1990, the United States had alerted or deployed force in situations short of war more than two hundred times.[44] Studies have shown that military force used in this fashion has generally been effective in the short term "to stabilize a worsening situation, to gain time, and even to defuse American demands for more drastic action..."[45] However, in the long term, force proved less effective. On the whole, these uses of force were better at deterring further action by an adversary than compelling the adversary to cease some activity; better at supporting friendly governments than at toppling governments or changing the policies of the adversary.[46] Consequently, these studies would lead us to expect the U.S. policies in Central America in the 1980s to have been less than successful, except in deterring outright invasions, or in shoring up the governments of Honduras and El Salvador for a few years.

The use of American force in Central America in the 1980s has to be considered long term, for it lasted for the entire decade and is still going on. Although deterrent successes are difficult to measure (Was the success due to the policy, or would it have happened anyway?), our deployments and continuing presence undoubtedly complicated the lives and plans of the Soviets, Cubans, and Sandinistas as they attempted to extend their own influence and that of their backward ideology. This is not inconsistent with what the data above might indicate. When the Sandinistas posed direct threats to stability, as they did in March 1986,

America responded with force short of war, acted in the short term, and produced the requisite deterrent. As for the fact that we also acted in the long term, and still seemingly produced astounding benefits . . . Well, the rules of the "science" of international relations often have exceptions. In exact accordance with the data above, though, our help certainly extended the life of the "friendlies" in the non-communist government in El Salvador, and provided the breathing space necessary for friendly democracy to take root in Honduras, and eventually even in Nicaragua.

The history of the use of force short of war would cause us to expect that attempts to compel changes in an adversarial state's government or policies are very likely to fail. Some of the persistent criticisms of our Central American policies centered around whether it was ethical, realistic, or worth the cost, exceedingly minor though the costs were to expect our actions to topple the Nicaraguan government, or to force a change in its sworn domestic and international programs. Yet, given the resounding electoral victory of the Chamorro coalition in early 1990 in Nicaragua, did our policies do just that? Did we compel a change in the Sandinista government? Probably not. Did we aid such an occurrence? Certainly. Indeed, many of the political left in America complain that the Nicaraguan Revolution never failed because it never had a chance to be fully implemented. It was hamstrung by American trade embargoes, aid restrictions, and military actions. I say "Hallelujah!"

This brings us back to the American military as a tool of policy. The results, the ends, of our military usage in Central America in the 1980s appear to be have been quite good. But what about the means and the tool itself? My diary accounts indicated problem areas. The military in Honduras in 1986 may have functioned like a well-oiled machine, doing every job that came its way, but the machine could run well while still having some weak parts and subsystems that were just waiting to fail if put under undue stress. Perhaps by looking too closely at the subject, analogous to looking at the skin of a beautiful person beneath a magnifying glass, the blemishes become too apparent. On the other hand, any military deployment serves as a case study for future improvements in the force, its personnel, training, and procedures. My perspectives were those of a midcareer, company grade Army officer, and suffered from the lack of experience available to older officers of higher rank. In the original edition, I offered suggestions on personnel and training that have been superseded by events – the aftermath of the Cold War, the Clinton Wars of the 1990s, and the War on Terror since 2001. Some suggestions – more language and culture training, a clear understanding of the strategic mission, and an institutional need to develop and track those with special training for low intensity environments – are still relevant.

In 1983, Lt. Gen. Wallace H. Nutting said of low- intensity conflict, "As a nation we don't understand it, and as a government we are not prepared to deal with it."[47] The organizational mind-set of the Army had been, of necessity, to prepare to wage heavy armored warfare in Central Europe and North Asia. Another mind-set of so many in the Army at that time was to equate low-intensity conflict with guerrilla warfare or counterinsurgency. While these types of conflicts are definitely part of the broad spectrum of LIC, they were by no means the only parts.

In most respects, the Army made substantial progress since my service in Honduras in 1986. As a lieutenant in the Engineer Officer Basic Course in 1984, I do not remember ever hearing of low-intensity conflict. When I attended the Engineer Officer Advanced Course in 1987, I was pleased to note that the course devoted a two-week module to LIC. The doctrinal instruction, though, was desultory at best. I was further disheartened to find out that the scenario we used for our capstone LIC exercise was an operation centered around Bandar Abbas in Iran. Our force would land to support the pro-American faction of the Iranian military operating in southern Iran. We would be opposing a force composed of Soviets and pro-Soviet Iranian units operating to the north. As the fighting centered on armored thrusts and the battle for air supremacy, it was quickly and painfully apparent that this was just the common European scenario transposed onto new geography. The competing factions of the Iranian military took the normal places of the NATO and Warsaw Pact allies.

Yet when I attended the Combined Arms and Services Staff School (known as CAS3) in the summer of 1990, a staff officers' course required of all Army captains before promotion to major, the situation had changed. The Army and the Air Force had significantly revised LIC doctrine, issuing a new FM 100-20 in 1990. Although we still conducted the obligatory war game focused on reinforcing and fighting in central Germany (less than a year after the fall of the Berlin Wall), the capstone exercise for the course was the deployment of a brigade-size task force to Honduras for the purposes of nation building. The doctrinal teaching and the exercise were done quite well.

The U.S. Army of the 1980s is long gone. Full-time military strength in the Reagan era peaked at 2.359 million in 1986, and dropped every year thereafter until 1999.[48] The Army went through a "draw down," losing about 40% of its strength. Absent the Soviet threat, the Department of Defense as a whole and the Army in particular, began emphasizing the potential of regional conflict as one of the primary organizing concepts for the future. Planners envisioned mid-intensity threats much like the Gulf War. Low-intensity conflicts were also given much more emphasis, as the planners presumed instability would continue to exist and threaten U.S. interests, even without Soviet meddling. In a general search for a "peace dividend," new missions were sought for the remaining military forces, from teaching high school mathematics to using nuclear submarines to track whales. Much of what had been called low-intensity conflict was re-named "military operations other than war," then "operations other than war." To enhance political appeal even further, armed incursions went under the name "humanitarian intervention" or "peace operations." With the return of "war," and the advent of the Afghan and Iraqi campaigns, more emphasis was placed on the broad term "stability operations," which in 2008 the Army placed on the same level as offensive and defensive operations.[49]

No matter the politically convenient nomenclature of the day, all of these operations still required the armed deployment of troops, generally to politically ambiguous missions and into unfamiliar social and cultural terrain. The content of training therefore must focus on the conduct, goals, and intermediate objectives of the overall effort, something that was lacking in the 1980s. The lowliest soldier now has to understand how the least incident of bad behavior matters. Among the necessary training are appropriate methods and behavior when dealing with the local population and the cultural taboos of the area; understanding the appearance of our own actions; understanding the reasons behind the mission and the unit's part in the action; recognition of the psychological mood swings likely to occur in the individual soldier— that eventually the soldiers are likely to come to resent the local population, or to see them as inferior, and this must be resisted; a frank discussion of the primitive conditions the soldiers are likely to be living in (and not to expect anything better). Most of all, they must be taught that even if there is combat, the killing of the enemy may not be the most important part of our overall efforts. Finally, in any situation, American forces have the right to self-defense. Hence, all soldiers, sailors, and airmen, regardless of sex, service, or branch must be expected to be proficient in basic weapons and tactics. We must also expect them to do the physical labor necessary to defend themselves. The grumbling and refusals to build bunkers and to stand guard that I observed in Honduras twenty-five years ago would be unacceptable today. Perhaps it happened in Honduras because we seemed so safe that the soldiers and their leaders saw little need for such an imposition on their time. This attitude was dangerous precisely because U.S. personnel did come to suffer from terrorist attacks in Honduras (see Appendix A). As our various enemies learned to exploit our vulnerabilities, asymmetric attacks against soft targets is the main threat nowadays to American personnel anywhere in the world.

The words of an earlier era of unpopular combat remain instructive: "For any man who wears his country's uniform, of whatever service, should be prepared to suffer, and if need be, to fight."[50] Fortunately, with the multiple deployments on lower intensity missions since the early 1990s, the Army has restructured the training at the National Training Center and at the Joint Readiness Training Center to prepare units in ways we would not have expected in the early days of JTFB.

In the 1980s, the American military was found to be useful again. Although the numbers in uniform were not much increased, the general quality of those serving rose. New equipment was provided and pay increased. Yet whenever a military is being refurbished, it means that it is intended to be used. The training of the forces guarding Germany and Korea was upgraded significantly, and troops spent more hours in the fields and classrooms.

The government also used armed forces in Beirut, Grenada,

Honduras, in the skies of Libya, in the waters of the Persian Gulf, and in the last two weeks of the decade, in Panama. As this book was originally being written, our nation had dispatched over 500,000 men and women to Saudi Arabia, sustained them there for months, and entered into war. Many experts in and out of service had been saying for years that post-Vietnam America did not have the national will, the training, the deployment capabilities, nor the quality of troops to do anything like this. The expectation among the "intellectuals" was that our plans would not work and that our high technology, bought from the lowest bidder by a scandal-ridden Pentagon contracting system, would fail miserably if it ever had to be used. Yet the training, technology, and the experience of the 1980s paid huge dividends by yielding a stupendous, unexpected, victory in the Gulf War at very low cost in allied lives.

The American military that I served with in Honduras carried a lot of emotional and cultural baggage. Whatever the residual glory of the Marne, Chateau-Thierry, Tarawa, Normandy, or Chosin, we also humped the memories of the Ia Drang, Tet, and My Lai. The latter were the heavier by far. Some of the old timers were fond of saying that John Wayne killed more GIs in Vietnam than the VC did. If that was true, then I was afraid that Hawkeye, Trapper John, B.J., Klinger, and Radar would kill far more in the next protracted ground war we might fight. I thought this would be so because we would have young soldiers whose Hollywood version of military service would be one of cynicism and disdain for the regimen required of a soldier. Regulations and routine might be seen as impositions, ridiculous manifestations of some "Mickey Mouse" system. I feared that if we got into heavy and protracted ground war in the Gulf that such weaknesses would come to the fore. I am pleased to note that, if not entirely groundless, my fears were not given the combat time to come to fruition in the Gulf War.

Yet, the spectacular success of Desert Storm should have provoked us to caution. Our operations in the Arabian deserts played to our strengths as a nation and to the strengths of the armed services as institutions. This was not a come-as-you-are war. Time, geography, technology, politics, and doctrine were weighted to our side. We had time to plan, assemble forces and staffs, study the enemy, and utilize our technology to the utmost— before hostilities began.

One of the most difficult chores in low-intensity conflicts was almost easy in Iraq and Kuwait in 1990-1991—the identification of targets. Our opposition was organized in large motorized or armored formations, arrayed in some of the most open terrain in the world. There was no jungle, heavy forest, or urban environment to hide in. The Iraqi armed forces, organized as they were, could not just blend into the local populace. These facts allowed our targeting and weapons technology a full range of employment, with devastating results. Given that most of the Iraqi forces were deployed in the barren, almost uninhabited lands of Kuwait and southern Iraq, there was no reason to hold back on our destructiveness. Compare this to the self-imposed restraints on our destructiveness and involvements in Southeast Asia, Central America, or in Iraq and Afghanistan today.

The Gulf War was also relatively simple in political terms. The invasion and rape of Kuwait made upholding Saddam Hussein as a champion against American imperialism very difficult indeed. On our side, the chief military and political goals were definable and gave a definite, reachable end to the conflict. They were, simply, to get the Iraqis out of Kuwait and restore the Kuwaiti government. This was a finite commitment, rather than the seemingly open-ended commitments often required in low-intensity conflicts.

Finally, we were challenged on the doctrinal grounds of our own expertise. The U.S. and European forces had been practicing for heavy, armored warfare for forty-five years. Our tactics and operational art had been honed for just this sort of conflict, with the exception that we had been practicing for the far more difficult, wooded terrain of central Germany, which is crisscrossed with numerous water obstacles, towns, and villages. Moreover, the U.S. forces had been practicing for most of the 1980s at the National Training Center (NTC) at Fort Irwin, California—a rugged desert environment. Some of the military experts on the news shows, and the columnists in the papers, during the Desert Shield portion of the operation were so bold as to suggest that our ground equipment, built for use in Germany, would not function well in the desert. Like so many of their colleagues in journalism, these pundits had forgotten, or perhaps had never bothered to learn, that the most significant upgrading of the armed forces in the 1980s had been in the realm of training. All of the major pieces of equipment in Army maneuver units had seen duty in the desert environment of the NTC.

Consequently, the U.S. forces had a strong cadre of soldiers and leaders who were no amateurs at either armored or desert warfare. Combine this with the fact that our units had time to study the enemy, focus unit training to ferret out individual and unit weaknesses, and, perhaps most importantly, get their minds straight on the dangerous job ahead. The combination was unbeatable.

But what we accomplished in the Gulf War did not tell us much about how our forces would fare if the targets were not so clear. What if the enemy could hide within the local populace? What if the commitment was for the grinding long term, with periods of hot and cold action, where the U.S. forces could not be easily isolated from a culturally different host population? What if we were fighting where the military and political goals were vague and the military tool was not preeminent, but ancillary to the diplomatic and the political tools? I would suggest that the Gulf War proved the deadly combination of good doctrine, good equipment, good troops, and simple, clear, limited missions. We saw this again in the ground war phase of Operation Iraqi Freedom.

The military of the eighties was peopled with generally committed soldiers, sailors, and airmen. They were smarter and better trained than any American force in history. It is the overall climate of the military that had changed. All of those things that once were considered military had been de-emphasized or diluted— whether in basic training where the drill sergeants no longer yelled epithets at the trainees, barracks life that resembled college-dorm life, or the fact that most soldiers fired their weapons only once a year. "Military" became militaristic, which became "hard core," which was informally taboo. Outside of a few elite units, it was no longer socially acceptable to concentrate on such things as killing. The emphasis was on technical accomplishment. Hence, it was doubly good that we had time to prepare in the Gulf in 1990.

As a training company commander in 1988-1989, I remember attending a mandatory seminar given by a civilian Ph.D. about how the military should train. His conviction was that since all we expected of basic soldiers was that they accomplish certain basic tasks, we should treat them like adults and ask them only to do those tasks—nothing else. He thought it was cruel to deprive trainees of candy bars, beer, and pizza, as long as they were proficient in their task accomplishment. As it was, we "deprived" the poor souls of their birthright to junk food for only four weeks. My comment to a senior drill sergeant (and Vietnam veteran) sitting next to me was "As long as task accomplishment is all that is important, then we should just send the trainee the lesson plans, give him a few months to learn the tasks in the comfort of his own home, then ask him to go down to the local recruiter to take his tests. Think of the billions we'd save."

"Right, sir . . ." was his caustic response.

Honduras called for technical competence, and we had plenty of it. But were we just civilians in uniform, reporting to a job that required longer hours and rougher living conditions than normal? Were we managers rather than leaders? I was certainly no better than the rest. Many times, I could have taken a stand against some stupid inanity of Palmerola life, but too often, I chose the easier way. We carried no weapons for the most part. Sometimes it seemed that we did not trust American soldiers with live bullets. We resisted bunker building and guard duty. Eventually, the same attitude says screw the helmet, screw fire discipline, why not sleep on ambush or guard duty? If there is any consolation, it seems that the essential becomes apparent when bullets start flying. But given America's records in so-called first battles, we lose a lot of good men in the learning process. However, we were at peace in Central America. The threat level was not high, and we were not front-line combat troops. We did have a profound effect, though, on the society we operated in—an overwhelmingly good effect despite some of the less savory aspects. We did our technical jobs well. The conflicts in Central America that we sought to influence by our presence were inherently political—and it was politics of the nastiest sort - civil conflict - where families and countries were turned inward against themselves. Consequently, any military response had to operate within that political spectrum.

For those reasons, the mixed force of medics, doctors, engineers, logisticians, and pilots at JTFB was the appropriate response short of war. We got in early. Our forces maintained a relatively low profile (it could have and should have been even lower). We paid attention to the local needs, said to be a breeding ground for insurgency—namely the material condition of life. Our efforts helped provide water wells, commercial roads, and schools. Our airstrips enabled doctors and teachers to reach hitherto isolated regions. Moreover, our presence demonstrated national commitment and resolve to staunch the spread of a dangerous ideology. Given the ambiguous nature of the conflict we were engaged in, perhaps it is fitting that the lessons were vague. Did we do well or poorly? Did we promote stability in the region, or did the stability come about in spite of our efforts? Did our presence actually hinder peace? My experience suggests that we were a force for good, peace, and stability: The Berlin Wall fell, and communism in Eastern Europe crumbled. Nicaragua finally had fair elections. Cuba remained isolated. The El Salvadoran rebels lost their main benefactors. Honduras remained stable.

Maybe we did our job better than anyone could have predicted. Whatever our shortcomings, the organizations and the people that continued to guard the jagged edges of freedom and to secure the free passage of the seas - a job passed down through the generations - always seemed to get the job done.

I went to Honduras in 1986 looking for something significant in my profession beyond sterile training exercises. Honduras gave me that significance. The American military operated there for real, for keeps. We were barely a thousand miles from our borders. Although we exhibited individual and organizational weaknesses, we functioned well in the aggregate and accomplished the purposes for which our nation sent us.

A song playing on a motivational film that was shown at the end of my Advanced Course graduation contained the refrain:

It wasn't always easy; it wasn't always fair.
But when freedom called, we answered. We were there.

Maybe it sounds corny, but that's the way I felt about serving in Central America, even for only six months. That's how I felt about serving my country in uniform. The "new" military just followed in the footsteps of the old. In so doing, we paid the next installment on the price of liberty. It is important to reflect that all too often freedom still proceeds from the barrel of a gun and that men and women can still find some nobility in sacrificing for their country and for noble ideals. Perhaps that was the real "*rumor of war*" in the late twentieth century.

POSTSCRIPT 2011

Joint Task Force Bravo is still operating at what is now called Soto Cano Air Base, more than 27 years after the initial deployments.[51] The critics of the mid-1980s- that predicted "permanence" for the U.S. presence in Honduras did so with a clear sense of foreboding.* To the critics, the U.S. presence in Honduras smacked of imperialism or interventionism dressed up as the latest coming of the bogeyman, "Vietnam." Yet, under President George H.W. Bush, "peacetime engagement" became the guiding national strategy. Under President Bill Clinton, this was re-christened "engagement and enlargement." These policies intended to keep America from withdrawing into itself after the Cold War by engaging with the newly freed nations in Europe and Central Asia, and with the "Emerging Markets" that were formerly known as the Third World or the Lesser Developed Countries. Through this continued engagement, the sphere of democracy and markets would be enlarged, and their benefits offered to more of the world. Furthermore, this engagement would include economic, diplomatic, informational, and military tools, depending on the situation. The military tool would promote respect for democracy and human rights, often through the sheer force of example. As such, the controversy over U.S. deployments in Central America disappeared from the front pages and the nightly news shows, although the military activities were little changed. The need to describe our activities in the mid-1980s as "training" rather than "operations," and as "temporary" was driven by the hyper-partisan domestic politics of the time, rather than any strategic needs of the U.S.

As events unfolded in Panama in 1989, the Gulf War, Haiti, Somalia, Bosnia, Kosovo and in the current War on Terror, American soldiers proved their ability to fight quickly, to fight well, and to perform a myriad of non-combat tasks. Twenty years of expeditionary deployments and nine years of continuous combat has led to a tactical focus in our armed forces that we simply did not have in 1986. Re-learning the fundamentals of counterinsurgency has now received years of effort, such

---

* See, for example, "A Big Brother for Honduras," *Newsweek,* 30 June 1986.

that some worry about American abilities to engage in heavier combat. Some of my observations on troop behavior and leadership, and the consequent recommendations that I made as a junior officer, have been resolved by the necessities of war. All of our troops today receive much better instruction on interacting with host societies. Deployed troops are generally armed with live ammunition, and thus are kept away from alcohol. Deployments on average are much longer than the 90- or 179-day deployments that seemed so onerous in 1986. Due to security concerns, and perhaps to avoid inciting local Muslim populations, R&R is taken outside the area of operations. Pornography is prohibited. Leadership at all levels has improved enormously, and as a result, so has general discipline. The JTFB operations of the mid-1980s relied heavily on medical, logistical, aviation, and engineer units, since the focus was not fighting. The experiences of our armed forces in the 1990s and 2000s also tell us that Military Police and other soldiers trained in providing general security to populations will also be heavily used, especially in any sort of "stability operation." While low-intensity conflict was a subject that struggled for attention in the 1980s, one could fairly argue that these missions now dominate the thinking of the Army and the Marines, and for much of the Air Force.

The military operations in Central America that were so controversial in the 1980s were ridiculously small in cost and troop levels, when compared to the much larger operations of the 1990s and 2000s. Yet, they were an important part of an American strategic process in Latin America that endured for decades through many Presidents, Republican and Democrat. The initiatives have taken different names – the Good Neighbor Policy, the Alliance for Progress, Enterprise of the Americas, Summit of the Americas – but the focus has been generally the same: supporting the development of civil society, democratic government and robust institutions, and the growth of the private sector. Use of force and the U.S. military has been but one of the tools, although often the most controversial tool. When I went to Honduras in 1986, a common refrain heard among intellectuals in classrooms, faculty lounges, seminars, and conferences was "Communism is the only real hope for Latin America," always expressed in quiet but serious tones. Revolutions, or Khrushchev's "wars of national liberation," were inevitable.

Thankfully, the intellectuals were wrong. Argentina, Bolivia, Brazil, Chile, El Salvador, Nicaragua, Guatemala, Haiti, Honduras, Panama, Paraguay, Peru, Suriname, and Uruguay transitioned from military or junta rule to democracy in the 1980s and 1990s. Chile, Peru, Brazil, and Mexico have since achieved investment grade financial status. Mexico and Chile have joined the Organization for Economic Cooperation and Development, whose 34 members are the world's most advanced economies that are committed to democracy and the market economy. Brazil went from being the world's financial basket case in the 1980s to one of the BRIC countries (Brazil, Russia, India, and China) that will define the 21st century world economy. Peru has experienced a decade of high economic growth. Chile has signed bilateral trade treaties with more than 100 countries and decided to teach all of its young to speak English. Panama, Costa Rica, and Trinidad have been called the "little tigers of the Caribbean" for their recent economic growth, which is reminiscent of the "Asian tigers" of the 1980s.[52] None of this progress was achieved by Soviet client states or through "people's revolutions." Indeed, if recent news stories can be believed, even the bloody, backward Marxist dictatorship of Cuba, held in such high esteem by Leftists in Europe and the U.S., is turning towards free markets after 50 years in darkness.[53]

Have poverty, corruption, and violence been eradicated in Latin America? No. Have Venezuela, Bolivia, Ecuador, and Nicaragua slid backwards economically, politically, and socially under the influence of Hugo Chavez, himself a former leader of a failed military coup? Yes. Has Argentina lost a decade under disastrous populist governments? Yes, but the tendency throughout the region is still headed in the right direction, and even in the backsliding countries, elections are still being held and the damage done to institutions, personal liberty, and private property is not yet irreversible. Honduras serves as an example that the return of authoritarianism in its leftwing variant is not inexorable. On 26 June 2009, the Honduran Supreme Court ordered the arrest of the serving president, Manuel Zelaya, for attempted violations of the Honduran constitution, and for ignoring earlier court orders. Defying the Court's order, the soldiers sent to arrest Zelaya on 28 June put him on plane to Costa Rica, rather than detain Zelaya for trial. Later the same day, the National Congress voted overwhelmingly to remove Zelaya from office for his constitutional violations. A majority of the Congress were members of Zelaya's own party, as was his constitutional successor, President of the National Congress Roberto Micheletti. Despite working for more than 25 years to strengthen constitutional processes and respect for rule of law in Honduras, the U.S. government backed Zelaya and demanded his return to power. The Honduran Supreme Court and the National Congress rebuffed the U.S. and other international demands for Zelaya's return, and proceeded with regularly scheduled elections in November 2009. Perhaps the pupils remained more faithful to the lessons than their former professors.

In the 2000s, one could encounter writings that alleged that the U.S. ignored Latin America as its focus turned to the Balkans in the 1990s and the War on Terror after 9-11. A strange turn of events, given that in the 1980s, the general intellectual thrust was to reduce alleged U.S. meddling in the region. In fact, as pointed out earlier, patterns of relations between nations have a tendency to endure, or repeat themselves. The U.S., by virtue of geography, cannot ignore the Caribbean Basin, or the Western Hemisphere. In the 1990s, the U.S. launched both the Enterprise of the Americas and the Summit of the Americas initiatives. In the 2000s, the U.S. launched the Free Trade of the Americas policy. These policies were backed by stronger stances in favor of increased commercial trade, and use of multilateral lending to reduce the heavy, inefficient, and often corrupt weight of state enterprises throughout Latin America, with substantial effect. In the 1990s and 2000s, Presidents Clinton, Bush, and Obama visited multiple Latin American and Caribbean countries and hosted many Latin American and Caribbean leaders in the U.S. Perhaps most importantly, in this period of alleged neglect, the U.S. signed and put into effect many free trade agreements: NAFTA (Canada and Mexico, 1993), CAFTA-DR (El Salvador, Guatemala, Honduras, Nicaragua, Costa Rica, Dominican Republic, 2004), Chile (2004), and Peru (2007), and negotiated free trade agreements with Colombia and Panama (still awaiting Senate approvals).[54] These are hardly the statistics of a foreign policy focused on ignoring Latin America. Moreover, when asked, four Central American and Caribbean nations sent troops to Operation Iraqi Freedom – El Salvador, Honduras, Nicaragua, and the Dominican Republic - which is an astounding achievement of U.S. foreign policy given where we had been less than 20 years previously.

The U.S. stood firmly for decades on the side promoting such progress, and we can be proud that we did so.

APPENDIX A

TERRORIST ATTACKS ON U.S. TROOPS IN HONDURAS, 1986-1990

8 AUGUST 1987. Bomb in Comayagua Restaurant. Occurred at 7:30 pm on a Saturday night. Five U.S. soldiers and one U.S. civilian hurt.

17 JULY 1988. Shooting in San Pedro Sula. A group of nine U.S. personnel had just boarded a small bus to leave a disco in San Pedro Sula. The attackers fired several shots into the bus and threw a grenade. Four U.S. personnel hurt.

2 FEBRUARY 1989. Attack on convoy. Assailants attacked a seven-vehicle convoy enroute to Yoro Province by firing five shots, hitting one vehicle. U.S. and Honduran security personnel were escorting the vehicles. No one was hurt.

18 FEBRUARY 1989. Bomb thrown at the liberty bus in Comayagua. Assailants hit the back of the liberty bus with a bomb as it was enroute between Comayagua and PAB. Three U.S. personnel were slightly injured. It was Saturday, again.

13 APRIL 1989. Attack on USAR/ARNG convoy. The convoy was enroute between PAB (by now renamed Enrique Soto Cano Air Base) and Yoro Province. Seventeen U.S. soldiers from the Regular Army, National Guard, and Army Reserves were involved. One vehicle was disabled by an explosive device.

13 JULY 1989. Bomb outside disco in La Ceiba. A convoy of vehicles enroute from road projects in the Aguan Valley to PAB had stopped to pass the night in La Ceiba. The leadership granted liberty to some of the soldiers. As one group was leaving a disco, an explosion occurred. Seven U.S. soldiers, all military policemen, were hurt, three of them seriously.

31 MARCH 1990. Sniper attack on bus. A group of U.S. personnel were

181

returning to PAB from an R & R excursion to Tela Beach. Assailants fired several shots into the vehicle. Six USAF personnel were hurt, two seriously.

NOTE: The incidents above indicate that the Honduran opposition groups learned that the easiest targets are GIs on liberty or GIs moving in easily identifiable vehicles along very restricted roads. The accounts above came from various American news reports of the incidents.

APPENDIX B

BALANCE OF POWER IN CENTRAL AMERICA, 1986

El Salvador
Total Armed Forces: 41,650
Army: 38,650
Navy: 650
Air Force: 2,350
Paramilitary: 18,000 including police forces and civil defence forces.
Foreign Advisors: 55 U.S.
Major Equipment: Army: 17 light tanks, 40 armored personnel carriers or reconnaissance vehicles, 56 pieces of artillery of various sizes. Most of the equipment is of U.S. manufacture. Navy: 20 patrol boats of various kinds. Air Force: 32 combat aircraft, 4 armed helicopters, 36 transport helicopters. Most are of U.S. or French origins.
Internal Opposition: about 10,000 organized among the various factions of the Marxist Frente Farabundo Marti de la Liberacion Nacional (FMLN).

Honduras
Total Armed Forces: 16,600
Army: 14,600
Navy: 500
Air Force: 1,500
Paramilitary: 5,000 belonging to the FUSEP who function as the nation's police force.
Foreign Advisors/support troops: about 1200 on average at Palmerola. Major Equipment: Army: 12 light tanks, 82 reconnaissance vehicles, 24 pieces of 105mm artillery. Most of the armored equipment is of British manufacture.
Navy: 9 patrol boats of various kinds. Air Force: 25 combat aircraft, 31 transport helicopters. Most are of U.S. or French origins.

Nicaragua
Total Armed Forces: 62,850

Army: 60,000
Navy: 850
Air Force: 2,000
Paramilitary: 45,000
Internal Opposition: 20,000 split in three forces. The Democratic Revolutionary Alliance (ARDE) had perhaps 2,000 fighters on the southern border. The Fuerza Democratica Nicaraguense (FDN), the faction that received most of the U.S. backing, had 15,000 operating along the northern border. In Miskitia, two mainly Indian factions were fighting with little more than 2,000.
Foreign military advisors: more than 3,000 from Cuba, East Germany, and the Soviet Union.
Major Equipment: Army: 122 medium tanks, 30 light amphibious tanks, 56 reconnaissance vehicles, 172 armored personnel carriers, 96 pieces of artillery of various sizes, 24 multiple- rocket launchers. The equipment was overwhelmingly of Soviet origin.
Navy: 28 patrol craft of differing origins. Air Force: 17 combat aircraft, 28 helicopters. Most of the airplanes were leftovers from the Somoza regime and were suited only for a counterinsurgency role. The helicopters included 12 Mi-8s and 6 Mi-24 Hinds from the Soviet Union. These helicopters are capable of being both troop transports and gunships. The Mi-24 is the most heavily armed helicopter in the world.

Sources: *The Sandinista Military Build-up* (Washington: U.S. Government Printing Office, May 1985). *The Military Balance, 1985-86* (London: International Institute for Strategic Studies, 1986) pp. 148-153.

Appendix C

MAJOR U.S. EXERCISE AND DEPLOYMENTS TO HONDURAS, 1983-1986

1983

Ahuas Tara (Big Pine) I: February 1983; Joint Honduran-American exercise including a Honduran Airborne operation using U.S. transports, joint counterinsurgency training, and medical civic action. Most of the activities occurred in northeastern Miskitia.

Ahuas Tara II: August 1983-February 1984; U.S. forces moved into Palmerola Airbase to establish a command-and-control center. This was a Honduran- American exercise that treated over 47,000 medical and dental patients and 37,000 animals; over 200,000 immunizations were administered and several wells dug. The U.S. Navy conducted maneuvers off the coasts of Honduras and Nicaragua, utilizing two carriers and the battleship USS New Jersey. The Marines conducted an amphibious assault on the northern coast of Honduras using two thousand marines and a battalion of Hondurans. Army engineers constructed eleven miles of tank traps in the Choluteca gap near San Lorenzo. Army and navy engineers constructed or improved airstrips at San Lorenzo, at the Regional Military Training Center at Trujillo, and at Aguacate in eastern Honduras. Special Forces units conducted counterinsurgency training with the Hondurans in the vicinity of Choluteca. Elements from the 101st Division artillery units deployed and conducted live-fire exercises with Honduran artillery units. U.S. personnel also installed a short-range-surveillance radar system (AN/TPS-63) on El Tigre Island (Tiger Island). In the midst of this exercise, the Grenada contingency operation and the bombing of the Marine barracks in Beirut occurred.

1984

Granadero I: March-June 1984; Honduran-El Salvadoran-American exercise focusing on military training objectives. Army engineers upgraded dirt airstrips at Cucuyagua and Jamastran. Troops from three nations participated in airmobile operations near Cucuyagua, on the El Salvadoran-Honduran border, and in an Airborne operation in the vicinity of Jamastran, near the Nicaraguan border. Observers from Guatemala and Panama also attended.

Ocean Venture '84: April-May 1984; Naval exercise in the Gulf of Mexico and the Caribbean. It involved scores of planes and ships and over 30,000 personnel.

Bigger Focus '84 also known as Post Granadero I: July-December 1984; a series of small deployment training exercises (DTEs, or deployments for training, DFTs); units included USAF, Navy, Army Rangers and Special Forces, medical units, and others. Commanders cited the minimum support available, language difficulties, and the remote, tropical terrain as being significant aids to the realism of training. (This period seems to be the starting point for the numerous small-unit DFTs, which continued from this period on.)

1985

Ahuas Tara III: February-May 1985; Honduran-American exercise combining armor and anti-armor exercises, engineering projects, and counterinsurgency exercises. Engineers upgraded or repaired the airstrips at San Lorenzo and Cucuyagua, drilled wells, and repaired and improved the antitank obstacles and fighting positions near Choluteca. U.S. armor units and the few Honduran tanks conducted combined maneuvers at Choluteca. Other combined forces conducted counterinsurgency training in Yoro Province.

Cabanas '85: June-October 1985; U.S. forces conducted counterinsurgency training and maneuvers with Honduran forces. Army engineers began turning a donkey path into a thirteen-mile stretch of road in Yoro province.

1986

Ahuas Tara '86: March-April 1986; essentially a command-post exercise (CPX) involving most of the contingency units in the U.S. armed services. Subordinate headquarters elements deployed to several locations in Honduras, while the center of the exercise was at Palmerola. The Sandinista incursion into Honduras as well as U.S. actions against Libya occurred while this exercise was underway.

Cabanas '86: March-May 1986; Phase I of this operation consisted of the 27th Engineer Battalion of the 20th Engineer Brigade from Fort Bragg parachuting into PAB to establish a support element. The rest of the battalion parachuted into Mocoron to build a dirt airstrip for use in the second phase. Phase II consisted of the 2d Battalion of the 75th Ranger Regiment from Fort Lewis conducting a mock Airborne assault on the dirt strip at Mocoron, and then conducting counterinsurgency patrolling with local Honduran units.

Blazing Trails '86: December 1985-June 1986; this was a continuation of the road-building project in Yoro Province. Engineers from the Missouri National Guard were in charge of this project. A new work force, essentially of battalion strength, rotated in every two weeks. This was a magnificent use of the Reserve Component of U.S. forces.

DFTs: During the first six months of 1986, nine engineer- related DFTs were conducted by units from the Army, Navy Seabees, and the Air National Guard. Several more DFTs also occurred involving active and re-serve units from other branches, such as the infantry Guardsmen from Arkansas.

NOTE: By 1986, U.S. forces had constructed or upgraded dirt airstrips at Cucuyagua, Aguacate, San Lorenzo, Puerto Lempira, and Jamastran. The paved runways at Palmerola and Trujillo also were extended, either by

U.S. forces or by contract. The upgrading of the hard-surface runway at Goloson Airfield near La Ceiba was underway in 1986. Additionally, U.S. forces normally performed civic-action programs and projects incidental to most combat training exercises.

SOURCES: The information above came from major American news accounts of the exercises as well as from *Welcome: A Guide for U.S. Participants in Combined Military Exercises in Honduras* (Fort Clayton, Panama: 193d Infantry Brigade Public Affairs Office, February 1985), chapter 3, and Bernard Eugene Harvey, *U.S. Military Civic Action in Honduras, 1982-1985: Tactical Success, Strategic Uncertainty* (Langley Air Force Base, Va.: Army-Air Force Center for Low Intensity Conflict, October 1988) pp. 15-19.

About the Author

Rick Waddell is a businessman currently living in Sao Paulo, Brazil. A native of Arkansas, he graduated from West Point in 1982, and holds advanced degrees from Oxford, Webster, and Columbia. He continues to serve in the U.S. Army Reserve.

Notes

[1] Martin Van Creveld, "The Human Dimension of Modern War," in *The Lessons of Recent Wars in the Third World,* vol II, ed. S. Neuman and R. Harkavy (Lexington, Mass.: Lexington Books, 1987), 87.

[2] As examples, see Michael T. Klare and Peter Kornbluh, eds., *Low Intensity Warfare: Counterinsurgency, Proinsurgency, and Antiterrorism in the Eighties* (New York: Pantheon, 1988) and D. Michael Shafer, *Deadly Paradigms: The Failure of U. S. Counterinsurgency Policy* (Princeton: Princeton University Press, 1988).

[3] After the end of the FMLN insurgency, the insurgents became politicians. Visit their website at http://www.fmln.org.sv/. In the elections of March 2009, the FMLN candidate won the presidential elections. From the standpoint of liberal democracy, this was a complete victory. In Nicaragua, the Sandinistas finally submitted to international pressure and held a truly open election in 1990, and their defeat came as an incredible surprise to their many sympathizers among the Western intelligentsia. In 2006, the former Sandinista junta leader, Daniel Ortega, was elected President, this time democratically.

[4] See *Honduras: A Country Study* from the Area Handbook Series (Washington, D.C.: Department of the Army, 1984).

[5] Alison Acker, *Honduras: the Making of a Banana Republic* (Boston: South End Press, 1988), 39.

[6] Ibid., 55.

[7] Ibid, 39-40.

[8] In the history of Mexico and Central America, liberals were generally the anticlerical forces seeking democratization and free institutions. The conservatives were generally pro-church and identified with authoritarian rule.

[9] Acker, 41, 44.

[10] See for example Hans J. Morganthau, *Politics Among Nations: the Struggle for Power and Peace,* 6th ed., revised by Kenneth W. Thompson (New York: Alfred A. Knopf, 1985), 7. Also, one of the current preeminent theorists of international relations simply states "The texture of international politics remains highly constant, patterns recur, and events repeat themselves endlessly." Kenneth N. Waltz, *Theory of International Politics* (New York: Random House, 1979), 66.

[11] As an example of this kind of thinking, see James Chace, *Endless War* (New York: Vintage Books, 1984). See also Walter LeFeber, *Inevitable Revolutions: The United States in Central America* (New York: W.W. Norton, 1983).

[12] Ibid., 23-24.

[13] Acker, 53.

[14] Acker, 54-55; Shirley Christian, *Nicaragua: Revolution in the Family* (New York: Vintage Books, 1986), 5-6.

[15] While at Oxford, the excellent sources assigned by my tutor covering Napoleon III and Maximilian included Alfred Jackson Hanna, *Napoleon III and Mexico: American Triumph over Monarchy* (Chapel Hill: University of North Carolina Press, 1971) and Hartford Montgomery Hyde, *Mexican Empire: the History of Maximilian and Carlota of Mexico* (London: MacMillan and Company, 1946).

[16] On these actions, see Gordon Connell-Smith, *The U.S. and Latin America* (New York: Wiley and Sons, 1974); Edwin Leuven, *U.S. Policy in Latin America: A Short History* (New York: Pager, 1965); Dana Munro, *Intervention and Dollar Diplomacy in the Caribbean* (Princeton, N.J.: Princeton University Press, 1964).

[17] For brief accounts of these actions see Capt. Harry Alanson Ellsworth, *One Hundred Eighty Landings of United States Marines, 1800-1934* (Washington, D.C.: Historical Section, U.S. Marine Corps, 1934). Most of the incidents were extremely minor, involving the landing of Marine detachments of a few dozen men to guard U.S. consulates or property.

[18] See Christian and John Norton Moore, *The Secret War in Central America: Sandinista Assault on World Order* (Frederick, Md.: University Publications of America, 1987) for general accounts of the march of Marxist-Leninism in Central America during this period.

[19] Bernard Eugene Harvey, *U.S. Military Civic Action in Honduras, 1982-1985: Tactical Success, Strategic Uncertainty* (Langley Air Force Base, VA: Army-Air Force Center for Low Intensity Conflict, October 1988), 62. Also *Welcome: A Guide for U.S. Participants in Combined Military Exercises in Honduras* (Fort Clayton, Panama: 193d Infantry Brigade Public Affairs Office, February 1985), chap. 3.

[20] John I. Alger, *Definitions and Doctrine of the Military Art* (West Point, N.Y.: USMA Department of History, 1979), 8.

[21] Headquarters Department of the Army, *Field Manual 100-20 Low Intensity Conflict* (Washington, DC: Department of the Army, January 1981), 14.

[22] Ibid., 31-32.

[23] Ibid., 75-77, 139-140. Note that little has changed in U.S. doctrine, since these are essentially the same set of principles used today in Iraq and Afghanistan.

[24] Captain Grant Steffan, "After Action Report—245th Engineer Detachment Deployment to Honduras," 15 April 1986, unpublished.

[25] Charles C. Moskos, *Soldiers and Sociology* (Evanston, Il: Northwestern University, 1988), 36-45. The quote is from 38-39.

[26] Ray Bonds, ed., *The Vietnam War: the Illustrated History of the Conflict in Southeast Asia* (New York: Military Press, 1979), 144.

---

[27] The World Council of Churches (WCC) sent official delegations to Managua in 1983 and 1985. They specifically denied any religious persecution had occurred in Nicaragua. The Sandinista government was called "a sign and transmitter of hope." In 1985, the WCC delegation contacted only the Sandinistas and pro-Sandinista groups in its visit. It also endorsed liberation theology. In this same time period, the WCC denounced only the United States by name as an oppressive interventionist power, despite the fact that Soviet aid to Cuba and Nicaragua was on the order of ten times the amount that the United States was providing to Latin America in its entirety. The U.S. National Council of Churches is a member of the WCC. In the mid-1980s, the WCC began to have its problems, caused in no small part by its support for violent revolution. Several members, such as the Salvation Army, canceled memberships. The source for the information recounted here is Earnest W. Lefever, *Nairobi to Vancouver: the World Council of Churches and the World, 1975-1987* (Lanham, Md.: University Press of America, 1987), 22-26, 72, 87. For the views of a liberation theologian, see the journal of the Brazilian bishop of Sao Felix do Araguaia, Pedro Casaldaliga, who visited the glorious Sandinista Revolution, published as *Prophets in Combat: the Nicaraguan Journal of Bishop Pedro Casaldaliga* (Oak Park, IL: Meyer Stone, 1987). In this book, the bishop declaims that "the cause of Nicaragua is the cause of all Latin America" (p. xii). He also talks about a "Gospel insurrection" and preparing people, as was being done by the Sandinistas, "who will devote their whole life, day in, day out, to God's Reign—which is grace and revolution—until death" (p. 67). He calls the Sandinistas and their supporters "real 'evangelizers' of peace and justice, servants of hope" (p. 98). Throughout, though, the bishop seems most impressed with internationalists like himself (someone once coined the name "Sandalistas" to describe these activists) who flocked to Nicaragua to support the revolution. For a journalistic account of church activism in the United States in 1986, see "Church Activists are on the March," *U.S. News and World Report,* 21 April 1986, 16-18. When the Sandanistas were voted out of office, and the FMLN sought peace, the leftwing church activists suddenly seemed to disappear, at least from the front pages.

[28] Daniel P. Bolger, *Americans at War: An Era of Violent Peace, 1975-86* (Novato, Calif.: Presidio Press, 1988), 444.

[29] T. R. Fehrenbach, *This Kind of War: A Study in Unpreparedness* (New York:

MacMillan, 1963), 622.

[30] Ibid., 564, 566.

[31] Dave Richard Palmer, *Summons of the Trumpet: U.S. Vietnam in Perspective* (San Rafael, Calif.: Presidio Press, 1978), 155.

[32] Ibid., 156.

[33] Moskos, 36.

[34] See Tien Dung Van, *Our Great Spring Victory:* An Account of the Liberation of South Vietnam, trans, by John Spragens, Jr. (New York: Monthly Review Press, 1977).

[35] See, for example, the assertions made by Louis A. Fanning in *Betrayal in Vietnam* (New Rochelle, N.Y.: Arlington House, 1976), 97.

[36] Jacqueline Sharkey, "The Tug of War: What Are We Really Doing in Honduras?" *Common Cause,* September/October 1984.

[37] "Temporary' Looks Like a Long Spell in Honduras," *U.S. News and World Report,* 2 June 1986, 28-29.

[38] "A Big Brother for Honduras," *Newsweek,* 30 June 1986, 37.

[39] See http://www.gao.gov/.

[40] Fred Hoffman, "Review of Panama Pool Deployment, December 1989," unpublished, March 1990, 17.

[41] President Ronald Reagan, "Statement on Signing the Immigration Reform and Control Act of 1986," 6 November 1986, http://www.reagan.utexas.edu/archives/speeches/1986/110686b.htm.

[42] For the unintended consequences of various immigration reforms, see Carolyn Lochhead, "A Legacy of the Unforeseen," *San Francisco Chronicle,* 7 May 2006, http://articles.sfgate.com/2006-05-07/news/17297061_1_immigration-

act-family-unification-immigration-expert. For the figures resulting from the 1986 Act, see "New INS Report: 1986 Amnesty *Increased* Illegal Immigration," Center for Immigration Studies, 12 October 2000, http://www.cis.org/articles/2000/ins1986amnesty.html.

[43] The World Bank estimates that total remittances from immigrants are $318 billion, of which $240 billion flows to the developing countries. See U.S. Joint Forces Command, *The Joint Operating Environment*, 18 February 2010, 17.

[44] Barry M. Blechman and Steve Kaplan, *Force Without War* (Washington, D.C.: Brookings, 1978), ix. Cited in Bruce Russett and Harvey Starr, *World Politics: The Menu for Choice,* 2d ed. (New York: W. H. Freeman, 1989), 168.

[45] See ibid, passim.

[46] Ibid., 168.

[47] U.S. Army, "Analytical Review of Low Intensity Conflict," *Joint Low Intensity Conflict Project Final Report,* vol 1 (Fort Monroe, Va.: TRADOC, 1986) 1-1.

[48] Anne Leland and Mari-Jana "M-J" Oboroceanu, "American War and Military Operations Casualties: Lists and Statistics," Congressional Research Service, 15 September 2009, 7.

[49] "Army Unveils New Stability Operations Manual," 6 October 2008, http://www.army.mil/-newsreleases/2008/10/06/13091-army-unveils-new-stability-operations-manual/.

[50] Fehrenbach, 346.

[51] Visit the JTFB website at http://www.jtfb.southcom.mil/.

[52] Duda Teixeira, "Os Tigrinhos do Caribe," *Veja On-Line*, 18 October 2006, http://veja.abril.com.br/181006/p_144.html.

[53] Many news articles began appearing in August and September 2010 about coming lay-offs of as many as 1 million Cuban state employees, who would be told to seek employment in a liberalizing private sector. See for example, "Raul

Castro: Cuba to Allow More Self-employment, Voice of America, 1 August 2010, http://www.voanews.com/english/news/americas/Cuban-Parliament-Convenes-Without-Fidel-Castro-99725094.html. In an interview with an American journalist in September 2010, even Fidel Castro admitted that the Cuban model no longer worked. See Paul Haven, "Report: Castro Says Cuban Model Doesn't Work," Associated Press, 8 September 2010, http://news.yahoo.com/s/ap/20100908/ap_on_re_la_am_ca/cb_cuba_fidel_ca stro_5.

[54] For a list of free trade agreements signed by the U.S., see http://www.ustr.gov/trade-agreements/free-trade-agreements.

CPSIA information can be obtained at www.ICGtesting.com
Printed in the USA
BVOW020946060712

294382BV00004B/33/P